The
EVERYTHING®
Chess Basics Book

Dear Reader:

Chess can be different things to different people. Some search for perfec-
tion and truth in each position. Some get addicted to competition and
strive to win. Some enjoy the mental exercise involved. Some like to play
a friend occasionally. Some like to follow the exploits of the grandmasters
of the game. Some like to delve into the theory of the game. Whatever
our take on chess, it is a game that has fascinated people for nearly
1,500 years and continues to fascinate people worldwide today.

    If you don't know what chess is or have a vague notion that it is a
board game, then this book will enrich your life by opening up the world
of what used to be called "the royal game." If you know enough about
chess to play an occasional game, but are not aware of the huge chess
subculture, you are in for a surprise.

    Like learning to play a musical instrument, learning to play and appre-
ciate chess opens up a whole new experience for anyone with enough
patience and perseverance to master the basics.

    I hope you enjoy this new experience for the rest of your life!

Welcome to the EVERYTHING® Series!

These handy, accessible books give you all you need to tackle a difficult project, gain a new hobby, comprehend a fascinating topic, prepare for an exam, or even brush up on something you learned back in school but have since forgotten.

You can choose to read an *Everything*® book from cover to cover or just pick out the information you want from our four useful boxes: e-questions, e-facts, e-alerts, and e-ssentials.

We give you everything you need to know on the subject, but throw in a lot of fun stuff along the way, too.

We now have more than 400 *Everything*® books in print, spanning such wide-ranging categories as weddings, pregnancy, cooking, music instruction, foreign language, crafts, pets, New Age, and so much more. When you're done reading them all, you can finally say you know *Everything*®!

QUESTIONS?
Answers to common questions

FACTS
Important snippets of information

ALERTS!
Urgent warnings

ESSENTIALS
Quick handy tips

PUBLISHER Karen Cooper

DIRECTOR OF ACQUISITIONS AND INNOVATION Paula Munier

MANAGING EDITOR, EVERYTHING SERIES Lisa Laing

COPY CHIEF Casey Ebert

ACQUISITIONS EDITOR Lisa Laing

DEVELOPMENT EDITOR Elizabeth Kassab

EDITORIAL ASSISTANT Hillary Thompson

Visit the entire Everything® series at *www.everything.com*

THE
EVERYTHING®
CHESS BASICS
BOOK

By the U.S. Chess Federation
and Peter Kurzdorfer

Endorsed by the U.S. Chess Federation

Adams Media Corporation
Avon, Massachusetts

To Caissa,
the goddess of chess, for her inspiration. —Peter

An Everything® Series Book.
Everything® and everything.com® are registered trademarks of F+W Publications, Inc.

Published by Adams Media, an F+W Publications Company
57 Littlefield Street, Avon, MA 02322 U.S.A.
www.adamsmedia.com

ISBN 10: 1-58062-586-X
ISBN 13: 978-1-58062-586-9
Printed in the United States of America.

J I H G

Library of Congress Cataloging-in-Publication Data
Kurzdorfer, Peter.
The everything chess basics book / The U.S. Chess Federation and Peter
Kurzdorfer.
p.   cm.   (Everything series)
ISBN 1-58062-586-X
1. Chess. I. United States Chess Federation. II. Title. III. Series.

GV1446.K87 2003
794.1–dc21

2003000371

This book is available at quantity discounts for bulk purchases.
For information, call 1-800-289-0963.

Contents

About the
U.S. Chess Federation

The United States Chess Federation (USCF) is the official governing body for chess in the United States, a not-for-profit organization dedicated to its 95,000 members. Since 1939 it has worked to promote the game of chess, providing a rating system for players, giving national titles, supporting chess teams in international play, and working to build scholastic chess competition in the nation.The award-winning *Chess Life* magazine is one important member benefit; affiliates receive the *USCF Rating List* six times a year, necessary to efficiently run chess tournaments. Many other publications are offered to USCF members. Another key member benefit: discounted prices on USCF's extensive product catalog offerings which include books, sets and boards, computers, software, teaching materials, and accessories (to request a *free* catalog please call ✆1-800-388-KING [5464] or shop online at *www.uschess.org*). USCF memberships are offered in twelve categories.

Internet chess is fast gaining popularity and USCF members can go to U.S. Chess Live (*www.uschesslive.org*) to play chess online. Chess Live features Grandmaster Simuls, "Battle of the Minds," Master Challenges, interactive chess exercises, rated tournament play, and more.
The World Chess Hall of Fame and Sidney Samole Museum has been located in Miami, Florida, since 2001. The Hall features chess history and houses a growing collection of artifacts comprising some of the world's most interesting and important pieces of chess history, such as the Paul Morphy silver beverage set and the playing table from the 1972 Fischer-Spassky match. (The Web site is *www.worldchesshalloffame.org*.) Sid Samole was a pioneer in the invention of the commercial chess computer. He founded Excalibur Electronics, a well-known manufacturer of chess computers and other electronic games, and is the benefactor of the Museum.

Acknowledgments

Thanks to USCF's Executive Director Frank Niro, Jami L. Anson, Jean Bernice, Tom Brownscombe, George DeFeis, Paula Helmeset, Al Lawrence, Kathleen Merz, Michele Stowe, Chess Author Bruce Pandolfini, and Hall of Fame Grandmasters Arthur Bisguier and Lev Alburt for their help, guidance, and patience. Thanks also to those wonderful modern inventions, the personal computer and e-mail.

Top Ten Reasons
to Learn the Game of Chess

1. You can build mental acuity through strategic play.

2. It's an easy-to-learn game that provides a lifetime of fun.

3. In existence for more than 1,400 years, chess is the most popular game in the world.

4. Chess doesn't depend on athletic ability—it's a game of mental skill.

5. You can learn to play at almost any age.

6. It's perfect for a rainy day!

7. Joining clubs will help you build your social circle.

8. Chess is one of the few games based solely on individual skills.

9. When you can't find an opponent, you can play online against the computer.

10. Impress your friends by beating them quickly!

Introduction

▶ CHESS IS A MENTAL EXERCISE that can be pursued for its own sake or for some other reason. The skills required to play a strong chess game include the ability to visualize, the ability to memorize, the ability to recognize patterns, the ability to use analytic logic, the ability to plan ahead, the ability to make decisions, and the ability to accept the consequences of your actions. Is it any wonder that chess is being touted as a useful subject for study in many schools?

Yet chess is nothing more than a board game. It has no inherent value beyond that. The previously mentioned skills are not necessary to play the game. They only become necessary if one is interested in playing chess well. This is comparable with skill in music. And like music, the casual player can appreciate superior skill in chess.

The Everything® Chess Basics Book is your introduction to the game that has challenged and fascinated so many people for so many years. In it you will learn a bit about the history of the game as well as some of the fascinating diversity available within the chess world. You will learn what chess is, how to read and write in the universal chess language, and how to play the game.

The meat of this book is in the middle, where all good chess players would expect to find it. (One of the basic principles of strong chess play is to control the middle of the board.) You can learn to play chess in one short session. It can take the rest of your life to really master its intricacies, but don't let that scare you away.

Don't expect that reading this book will make you a strong player. It won't. Instead, you are shown the many building blocks that are the foundation of good chess play. These building blocks are strategic and tactical principles that allow you to pick out a plan based on the pawn structure or find a combination based on your awareness of an exposed king and a couple of tactical patterns. You are shown what the pieces can do singly and in combination, and given guidelines to think about regardless of the position you might find your pieces in.

These basic principles are the hallmark of the strong player. They were discovered over several hundred years by many chess pioneers and are the property of all modern chess masters. But they are really nothing more than an expression of the inherent logic of the game. For example, the great strength of the fast-moving bishop is its ability to get from one place to another in a hurry. Therefore, a bishop that cannot get anywhere at all, much less in a hurry, is something to be avoided. Thus you try to saddle your opponent with a bad bishop, while trying to get rid of your own bad bishop.

After learning the basic principles of chess, you should be able to enjoy playing over the games of the masters, appreciating the nuances they employ to make their ideas work. You should also be able to enjoy a game with almost anyone, even if that only means understanding why your position is bad.

Once you have mastered the basics, it's up to you how far you want to progress at chess. So enjoy the game in whatever way you like. Your life will thereby be enhanced. Ⓔ

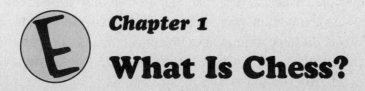

Chapter 1

What Is Chess?

Chess is a strategic game designed for two players who battle each other with an army of sixteen chess men each. The bottom line of the game is to keep your king from being checkmated while trying to checkmate your opponent's king.

Early Chess

Chess is a descendant of a game called Chaturanga believed to have originated in India in the sixth century and which may have been related to a much older Chinese game. Writings about this oldest form of chess were found around A.D. 600.

Chaturanga is a Sanskrit word that refers to the four arms of the old Indian army—elephants, cavalry, chariots, and infantry—from which come the four types of pieces in that game. Checkmate may come from the ancient Persian phrase *shah manad*, meaning "the king is helpless [or defeated]."

Early Forms of Chess

Chaturanga spread eastward from India to China and then through Korea and Japan. It appeared after the Islamic conquest (A.D. 638–651) in Persia, where it was first called Chaturanga, and then Shatranj, which is the Arabic form of the word. The spread of Islam to Sicily and the invasions of Spain by the Moors brought Shatranj to Western Europe. It reached Russia through trade from several directions.

Chess seems to have spread rapidly along the routes of commerce: first to Persia, then to the Byzantine Empire, then throughout the rest of Asia. By the end of the tenth century, the game was well known throughout Europe and had attracted the serious interest of kings, philosophers, and even poets.

Muslims, it seems, welcomed chess, and the Arabs extensively studied chess, analyzed games, and wrote in great detail about chess. The Arabs probably developed the algebraic notation system (see Chapter 6).

Europe Embraces the New Game

Chess reached Europe probably between the seventh and ninth centuries. Excavations at a Viking grave site off the south shore of Brittany have uncovered a chess set; tenth-century chess figures of Scandinavian origin, still made in the traditional Arabic form, have been excavated at Vosges, France. In the Middle Ages, chess was played according to the Muslim rules with the queen and bishop as comparatively weak pieces, able to move only one square at a time.

In the twelfth and thirteenth centuries, puzzle solving in chess became a particular pastime—for example, finding a solution such as a forced checkmate in a given number of moves. Overall, strategies became more refined as knowledge of how to play at higher levels was passed down and built upon.

Subsequently, Italians began to rule the game, wrestling the supremacy of the game from the Spanish. Then came the French and the English during the eighteenth and nineteenth centuries, when chess spread among the common folk—until then the game was principally played by royalty and the aristocracy. With the public now playing chess, the level of play improved considerably. Matches and tournaments were played with great frequency, and prominent players of the game developed schools and followers.

Modern Chess

The game of chess as it exists today emerged in southern Europe toward the end of the fifteenth century. Some of the old Shatranj rules were modified, and new rules were added.

Rule Changes

Toward the end of the fifteenth century, modern chess became more strategic and comprehensive—when pawn promotion upon reaching the eighth and last rank and castling, in which a player could more quickly defend his or her king, was added. The implementation of the "en passant" (in passing) rule permitted pawns to move two squares forward on the first move.

In the sixteenth and seventeenth centuries, chess took another huge leap. As the game increased in popularity, chess started to become more refined and more strategic and was modified to reflect that refinement.

The purpose was to increase the complexity of the game and also to create a greater opportunity for maneuverability for opponents to explore a wider range of strategic options.

The most notable changes turned the *fers* (counselor), a weak piece in Shatranj, into the queen, which became the most powerful piece. Also, the *alfil*, which moved in two-square steps, was changed to the bishop and enabled to move in a more far-ranging manner.

FACT

This "new" game gained popularity all over Europe and by the sixteenth century the best players were recording their games and theories in widely circulated books of chess instruction and notation.

Leading Players

In the eighteenth century, François André Danican Philidor, a Frenchman, was the leading player of his time. In 1749 he published *L'analyse du jeu des Échecs,* or "Analysis of the Game of Chess," which was one of the most influential theoretical works of its time. Philidor was the first to analyze many of the main strategic elements of chess and to recognize the importance of proper pawn play.

French players continued their dominance of the game long into the nineteenth century. In 1834, Louis Charles de la Bourdonnais played a series of six matches in London against the then-best English player, Alexander McDonnell. Bourdonnais soundly defeated McDonnell—he won forty-five games and lost thirty-two with thirteen draws by all accounts. The games played in these matches were published and analyzed worldwide.

In 1843, English player Howard Staunton decisively defeated the leading French player, Pierre Charles de Saint-Amant. This victory placed Staunton as the nineteenth century's foremost chess player with a score of eleven wins, six losses, and four draws. Staunton also wrote several theoretical works on chess and commissioned the design for chess pieces. Though there are many variations on chess piece design, the

Staunton chess pieces are today's standard and are widely used by beginners and experienced players alike. The pieces are known as *Staunton Chessmen*. Staunton also organized the first international chess tournament, held in London in 1851. German player Adolf Anderssen won the tournament.

The Fédération Internationale des Échecs

As global presence of chess increased, it became evident that an international chess organization was needed. The Fédération Internationale des Échecs, or FIDE (pronounced FEE-day), was established and since 1924 has been a force for unification and world standards. FIDE maintains a numerical rating system for master players, awards titles, organizes the world championships, and runs a chess Olympiad every other year that brings together teams from dozens of countries.

FACT

The first international chess tournament was the London Tourney of 1851, won by Adolf Anderssen of Germany. Anderssen then became known unofficially as the world's best chess player even though he did not receive an award or title. International tournaments caught on, and they have been mushrooming ever since. Today there is some international tournament—sometimes more than one—taking place every day of the year.

American Chess

The first great American chess player was Paul Morphy. Morphy consistently demonstrated his superiority over his American rivals, and in 1858 traveled to Europe to prove himself against the world's finest players. Within six months of his arrival, he had won matches by overwhelming scores against several prominent players, including Anderssen. Because of his youth and the extraordinary quality of his games, Morphy was hailed as a genius and was recognized as the best chess player in the world. Sadly, Morphy's chess career ended upon his return to the United States. He became mentally ill and never again played competitive chess.

FACT

The first national open events were played in Kentucky when Paul Morphy, the first great American-born chess player, was still a child. Morphy, of Irish ancestry, lived in the Civil War era. He traveled to Europe in the 1850s, beating all challengers, including Adolf Anderssen. However, the English champion of the time (Howard Staunton) refused to play a match, so Morphy became despondent. It is generally conceded today, and at the time as well, that Morphy would have won such a match convincingly.

Influential Americans

In the early twentieth century, several Americans were influential in the chess world. Harry Nelson Pillsbury, born in Somerville, Massachusetts, in 1872, was one of the best players in the world during his brief career. Frank Marshall of New York City was one of the strongest players in the world and was U.S. champion for decades. Marshall founded the famous Marshall Chess Club in New York City and encouraged many young players.

Kenneth Harkness, who was born in Scotland, invented a numerical rating system for chess players that is essentially still in use today. George Koltanowski, born in Belgium, was a kind of latter-day Johnny Appleseed of the chess world. He traveled the country during the Depression and afterward, running Swiss-system tournaments, teaching chess, and giving blindfold exhibitions. He was a key figure in popularizing chess in the United States.

Oversees Again

In the mid-nineteenth century, the center of chess activity returned to Europe after Morphy's heyday and produced several outstanding players. Wilhelm Steinitz, Siegbert Tarrasch, Emanuel Lasker, and many others advanced the theory and practice of chess through their games and writing.

Additionally, chess had been very popular in Russia, and after the Russian Revolution in 1917, the Communist government began a program of chess education for children. The government also sponsored many chess events and provided financial support for its best players. Because of the emphasis put on chess by the Communist government and the fact that the habit of extensive chess education and strong chess play is in their blood, players from the former Soviet Union have been able to focus their efforts on winning chess, and thereby have long dominated international chess.

Today, the highest levels of world chess are still dominated by players trained under the Soviet system. However, the dominance of these players is being threatened by a new influence on the game: computers.

Computer Chess

The first computer programs that could play chess emerged in the 1960s. Although the programs played according to the rules, they were easily defeated. However, as computers became more sophisticated, so too did the games they could be programmed to play. This rapid improvement allows today's computer chess programs to beat today's top players.

Human Versus Computer

In the 1970s, English international master David Levy made a bet with some computer programmers that no computer could defeat him in a chess match within ten years. He won the bet by defeating the best program they could throw at him and renewed the bet for another ten years. He won again. But then computers started to gain some real playing strength, and Levy wisely quit while he was ahead.

In the 1990s, IBM computer scientists developed a chess computer they named Deep Blue. Deep Blue was able to analyze millions of chess positions every second. In 1996, in a highly publicized match, world chess champion Garry Kasparov defeated the computer four games to two. Kasparov faced an improved version of Deep Blue called "Deeper Blue" the following year in a rematch.

In the event marked as the first-ever serious defeat of a world chess champion by a computer, Kasparov won the first game of the rematch, but drew Deeper Blue in games three, four, and five, and lost to Deeper Blue in games two and six. Kasparov, who it is said is capable of analyzing an amazing three positions per second, couldn't overcome Deeper Blue's ability to process 200 million positions per second.

Three positions per second works out to an amazing 180 positions per hour. That's the amount of positions Kasparov supposedly can process. But it isn't his speed so much as his ability to accurately assess each position that makes Kasparov, or any human champion, such a formidable foe of a computer that can look at millions of positions per second but cannot assess them very well.

Other Uses for Chess Computers

Playing chess is not the only thing chess computers can do. A computer is a very sophisticated instrument, and there are programs out there that can teach you how to play chess and coach you to play better chess. There are large databases that store millions of chess games and positions. There are CDs that do all of the above.

There is also the Internet, of course. Chess Web sites abound, and playing over the Internet and via e-mail has become a quite popular modern activity. Computers have made a big impact on the royal game.

World Chess Champions

In 1886, a match was held between Wilhelm Steinitz from Prague (now the capital of the Czech Republic) and Johann Zukertort from Poland. The match was held to specifically decide who could legitimately claim the title of world chess champion. Each man had achieved great success in previous tournaments and matches. Steinitz had defeated Zukertort in an 1872 match, but Zukertort won the great London tournament of 1883 ahead of Steinitz. Steinitz won the 1886 match decisively with ten wins, five losses, and five draws, thus becoming the first official world chess champion. (Although Anderssen and Morphy were both considered at times to be the world's strongest player, neither was given an official title.)

Lasker to FIDE

Emanuel Lasker, a twenty-five-year-old German player, took the world champion title from Steinitz in 1894. Lasker held it a record twenty-seven years and was deposed as champion in 1921 by Cuban master Jose Raul Capablanca. Russian-born Alexander Alekhine of France dethroned Capablanca in 1927. Alekhine lost the championship to Dutch player Machegielis (Max) Euwe in 1935, but was able to regain it in a rematch just two years later. When Alekhine died in 1946, he was still the reigning champion, so FIDE set out to find a new champion. In 1948, FIDE organized a special competition among the world's five best players. Mikhail Botvinnik of the USSR won the title.

FIDE had been founded in 1924, but it wasn't until Alekhine's death in 1946 that the organization was able to take control of the world championship.

Soviet Champions

Since 1948, FIDE championship matches have been held every few years. Botvinnik reigned as world champion for almost fifteen years, even though he lost world championship matches to two Soviet players—to Vassily Smyslov in 1957, and in 1960 to Latvian Mikhail Tal, who was then twenty-two. But each time he lost a world championship match, Botvinnik exercised his right to a return match, and each time he convincingly won the return match. He defeated Smyslov in 1958 and Tal in 1961 to recapture the world championship. Then, after Botvinnik lost to the Armenian Tigran Petrosian in 1963, FIDE announced that the rematch clause was revoked. Botvinnik promptly announced his retirement from championship play.

A Six-Month-Long Match

The Russian Boris Spassky defeated Petrosian for the world championship in 1969, but then in 1972, Bobby Fischer defeated Spassky. Fischer was the first American world champion and the first non-Soviet to win a world championship under the FIDE rules adopted after 1945.

When Fischer declined to defend his title in 1975, Anatoly Karpov began a ten-year reign as world champion. The first title match between Karpov and Garry Kasparov in 1984 to 1985 was halted after it had lasted six months without producing a winner. Karpov had won five games, Kasparov had won three, including the last two in a row, and there were forty draws. Thus the score of the match was twenty-five to twenty-three when the match was halted.

The world championship matches had traditionally been played over a limited number of games, usually twenty-four, with a winner declared after scoring 12½ points. If the match was drawn, the champion retained the title. Largely because of protests by Bobby Fischer, the rules were changed for the 1975 match, with the champion now decided by the first player to win six games. Therefore, a match could go on quite a long time if many games ended in draws.

FACT

Points are scored in chess tournaments or matches by winning or drawing games. A win counts as 1 point, a loss counts as 0 points. A draw counts as ½ a point for each player. Thus, in order to gain 12½ points in a match, a player has to score some combination of wins and draws that add up to 12½, such as 6 wins and 13 draws.

Fischer refused to defend his title in 1975 despite the rule changes. But the biggest reason the rules were finally switched back was because of the six-month-long 1984 match between Karpov and Kasparov.

Then-president of FIDE, Florencio Campomanes, said at the time he was trying to protect the health of the players, whom he said "looked exhausted." But Kasparov said he felt that Campomanes wanted to save the title for his friend Karpov. In their next match in 1985, Kasparov defeated Karpov for the title and subsequently defended the title against him three times.

Professional Chess Association

However, the controversy was not yet over and resulted in Kasparov and Nigel Short separating from FIDE. In 1993, Kasparov and his official challenger, Nigel Short of England, rejected FIDE's proposed arrangements for their world championship match. They set up a rival organization, the Professional Chess Association (PCA), and hoped to gain commercial sponsorship and television coverage on a much larger scale than FIDE was able to accomplish.

In May 2002, in the city of Prague, FIDE reached an agreement with the world's top-ranked players for a reunification of the world chess championship. Braingames World Champion Vladimir Kramnik will play a match against the winner of the Dortmund candidates' tournament, Grandmaster Peter Leko. Simultaneously, FIDE World Champion Ruslan Ponomariov will play a match with the world's top-rated player, Garry Kasparov. The winners of each of these matches will play a match for the undisputed World Chess Championship title.

Kasparov defeated Short under the auspices of the PCA and claimed the title of world champion. But Karpov had remained loyal to FIDE and also claimed the title after winning a FIDE-sanctioned match against Jan Timman of the Netherlands, despite the fact that he had earned this right because he had lost matches to both Short and Kasparov over the previous two years.

The split remained for the rest of the 1990s, and Kasparov successfully defended his PCA title against Viswanathan Anand of India in 1995. However, Kasparov resigned as president of the PCA, and it quickly fell apart without his leadership. FIDE once again took the reigns and sanctioned a new world championship in a new "knockout" format. Participants were seeded in a large draw and had to advance through a number of rounds in a short time.

Karpov won the first title under this format, after getting seeded into the final match, but later was unhappy with the tournament arrangements when he lost the special privilege of being seeded into the finals. In 1999 he

THE EVERYTHING CHESS BASICS BOOK

refused to participate, and Alexander Khalifman of Russia took the FIDE title. In 2001 another knockout world championship was held, and the eighteen-year-old Ukrainian grandmaster Ruslan Ponomariov won the event.

After five years without holding a title challenge, Kasparov was finally able to secure sponsorship for a world championship contest of his own in 2000. (The sponsorship Kasparov got for this championship was provided by BrainGames. Thus the 2000 championship was billed as the BrainGames World Chess Championship.) But he lost the match to his former student, twenty-five-year-old Vladimir Kramnik of Russia. Kramnik was chosen as the challenger because he was the second-highest-rated player in the world at the time.

The United States Chess Federation

The United States Chess Federation (USCF) was established in 1939 to advance the role of chess in the United States. The USCF serves as the governing body for chess in American society and promotes the study and knowledge of chess. It also organizes tournaments, sanctions thousands of tournaments, and rates over a half-million games each year. Top events include the U.S. Championship, U.S. Women's Championship, U.S. Amateur Championship, U.S. Junior Championship, and U.S. Senior Championship. The USCF publishes the *U.S. Chess Federation's Official Rules of Chess* for chess play in the United States and sponsors American player participation in international events such as the World Chess Olympiad and the World Chess Championship. The USCF is the official sanctioning body for American players who want to qualify to compete in FIDE events.

Chess was one of the first three sports to form a national organization in the United States, which was the second nation to form a national chess organization. Paul Morphy of New Orleans was the first American to be recognized as the world's best player, and Bobby Fischer was the first American to win the official title of world chess champion.

Under the auspices of the USCF, players of all strengths, from novice to grandmaster, can play chess in any number of ways—OTB (over the board), correspondence chess, or online (computer chess through the Internet)—although for competitive purposes, the USCF only recognizes OTB and correspondence chess.

There are also magazines and Web sites available for every conceivable subgroup in chess: problems, correspondence chess, speed chess, specific openings, grandmaster game collections, history, and chess set collections are a few of the subjects available.

The USCF is a national organization built up from the grassroots. State organizations and regional organizations oversee a lot of chess activity, and local clubs and individuals contribute a great deal to its health as an organization. Many state organizations and even some chess clubs have their own magazine and Web sites, which are a wonderful complement to the USCF's own magazines, *Chess Life* and *School Mates*, and its Web site, ✐ *www.uschess.org.* Ⓔ

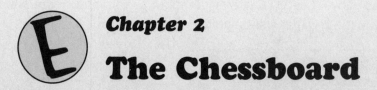

Chapter 2

The Chessboard

The game of chess takes place on a square board divided up into sixty-four smaller, equally sized checkered squares alternately colored light and dark. While the board can be almost any size and the squares can be almost any color, it is best to keep within the standard size of about 16 to 22 inches to a side for the board with 2 to 2½-inch squares.

The Battlefield

Everyone has sixty-four squares to work with. Half of sixty-four is thirty-two. Therefore, a rule of strategy immediately springs to mind: If you control thirty-three squares, you will have an advantage. Thus you already have an idea of how to plan an attack before you know how the pieces move. Keep this strategy in mind as you learn more about chess, and the rewards will be gratifying.

◄ Here is a diagram of a chessboard. Note the checkered squares and the light square at the right-hand corner at the bottom.

Light on Right

When setting up the chessboard, always make sure a light square is at your far lower right corner. Your opponent, who sits opposite you, will also have a light square at his or her far lower right corner. (If you prefer, you can think of this as a dark square always being at your left; it works just as well.) There is perhaps no reason other than tradition for this rule, but it makes sense to always set the board up the same way for all chess games.

You should be able to spot the many instances where chess is used in advertising without a modicum of research. Look around you at store windows, magazine ads, posters, television shows, and movies. Notice how many chessboards are set up with a dark square in the lower right-hand corner. You have found another case of homework gone undone!

Blind Your Opponent

An old piece of advice to chess players came up in a sixteenth-manuscript by the Spanish bishop Ruy Lopez. He counseled his readers to place the board so that the sun shines in their opponent's eyes. Not a very nice bit of advice, but how nice can you be when the object of a game is to destroy your opponent? Nevertheless, such behavior is considered unsportsmanlike nowadays.

Following the principles of good sportsmanship, the board should not have shiny squares. A smooth surface, easy on the eyes, with lots of contrast between the light and dark squares, is ideal.

FACT

The material of a chessboard can be almost anything. Wood, plastic, paper, cardboard, and vinyl are common. Some chessboards are even virtual: they appear only on your computer screen. So long as there are sixty-four alternating light and dark squares, you have a useable board.

Checkered Squares

The distinctive appearance of the chessboard, aside from the sixty-four-square grid, is the alternating light and dark squares. This is so unique that any time a checkered pattern appears with contrasting light and dark colors, people automatically think of a chessboard (or checkerboard, which is really the same thing).

QUESTION?

Has the chessboard always been checkered?
The surprising answer is no. Older versions of chess in India and the Middle East were played on a board with the grid dividing it into sixty-four squares, but without contrasting colors.

The colors of a chessboard can be whatever you like as long as they offer good contrast between the light and dark squares. The red and white of the traditional checkerboard is a bit gaudy. Better is the soft green and beige of many vinyl roll-up boards or the walnut-maple squares of some wood boards.

Using All Squares

In chess, both players use all the squares of the board. This is in contrast to the many versions of checkers, in which each player uses only half of the squares. It also gives special meaning to the appearance of the chessboard in terms of game planning. There are advanced strategies known as *weak-color complexes*, where a player cannot get sufficient control of the squares of one particular color. There is even a chess piece that operates on only one color, which you will learn about in the next chapter.

Preventing Visual Monotony

There is one other reason for the alternating light and dark squares on the chessboard: It prevents a visual monotony, thus helping players to quickly and accurately distinguish between the various squares on the board. To go along with this, it allows players to easily visualize the various highways that cross the board.

The squares of the chessboard do not exist in isolation. They touch or intersect at various points. Straight rows of such bordering squares are called *ranks*, *files*, and *diagonals*.

Ranks

As you sit at the chessboard, with a light square at your lower right and a dark square at your lower left, there are eight horizontal rows of eight squares bordering at the sides stretching from your left to your right. They begin nearest you and wind up nearest your opponent. These rows cover every square on the chessboard, and they are called *ranks*.

Rank Names

Each rank has a name based on how far away it is from you, assuming you are playing the White pieces and your opponent is playing the Black pieces. The rank nearest you is called the *first rank*. The next rank out is called the *second rank*, the next the *third rank*, and so on until you get to the rank nearest your opponent, which is called the *eighth rank*. If you are playing the Black pieces, the rank nearest you is the eighth rank and the rank nearest your opponent is the first rank.

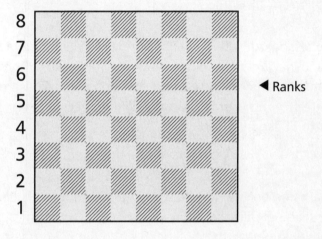

◀ Ranks

Rank Properties

Each rank contains four light squares and four dark squares, which naturally alternate. Each light square borders on a dark square, and each dark square borders on a light square.

It's not enough to place the board with a light square in the right-hand corner. You also have to set up the White pieces on the first rank and the Black pieces on the eighth rank. Otherwise it will become very difficult to keep score of a game; something you will learn to do shortly.

All ranks are not equal. Notice that the first and eighth ranks each border only one rank, while all the other ranks border two ranks. The edge of the board can be a severe restriction in chess, and the first and eighth ranks represent part of that edge.

White sets up his pieces on the first rank and his pawns on the second rank, while Black sets up her pieces on the eighth rank and her pawns on the seventh rank. (The chess pieces consist of the kings, queens, bishops, knights, and rooks. They are all taller and stronger than the little pawns.)

Files

As you sit at the chessboard, with a light square at your right and a dark square at your left, there are eight vertical rows of eight squares bordering at the sides and stretching between you and your opponent. These rows of eight squares stretch from your left to your right and cover every square of the board. These rows are called *files*.

File Names

Each file has a name beginning with a letter and ending with "file." Assuming you are ready to play the White pieces, counting from your left the files are the a-file, the b-file, the c-file, and on to the file furthest to your right (the one with the light square), which is the h-file.

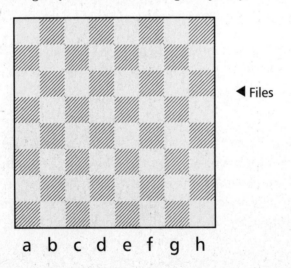

◀ Files

a b c d e f g h

Assuming you are ready to play the Black pieces, counting from your left the files are the h-file, the g-file, the f-file, and on to the file furthest to your right (the one with the light square), which is the a-file.

Where ranks and files intersect at a square, there is also a name. On a chessboard, find the a-file and the fifth rank. The dark square there is called a5. Now find the e-file and the fourth rank. The light square you are looking at is e4.

File Properties

Each file contains four light squares and four dark squares, which naturally alternate. Each light square borders on a dark square, and each dark square borders on a light square.

There are an equal number of light squares and dark squares on the chessboard: thirty-two for each. Place the board like a diamond and you will see them lined up in vertical and horizontal rows. These are commonly referred to as *diagonals*.

All files are not equal. Notice that the a-file and the h-file each border only one file, while all the other files border two files. The a-file and the h-file represent the other part of the edge of the board. (The first and eighth ranks also represent the edge of the board.)

Diagonals

Ranks and files are not the only highways of the chessboard. There are also the diagonals, which are straight lines made up of individual squares that border at the corners, rather than at the sides. They appear to stretch out at an angle from the players' perspective.

The following three main things distinguish a diagonal from a rank or file.

1. Diagonals border at the corners rather than at the sides.
2. Diagonals come in a variety of sizes, whereas ranks and files always contain eight squares each.
3. Diagonals consist of squares of one color only, whereas ranks and files always contain an equal mixture of dark and light squares.

Diagonals do not have easy-to-remember, simple names like ranks and files do. But they are sometimes named for the first and last square on the diagonal: the long dark diagonal can be called the a1-h8 diagonal, while the smallest light-square diagonals can be called either the h7-g8 diagonal or the a2-b1 diagonal.

Border

Diagonals border at the corners rather than at the sides of the squares that make them up. This brings up an interesting optical illusion. Look at a chessboard. Consider the a-file and a1-h8 diagonal. Which is longer?

If you answered the diagonal, you were right in a strictly geometrical sense, but wrong in a chess sense. Each row contains eight squares, and that means that they are the same size for the purpose of a chess game. By the same token, it might look like the b1-h7 diagonal is longer than the b-file. But actually it is the file that is longer! The b-file, like all files, contains eight squares, whereas the b1-h7 diagonal consists of only seven squares.

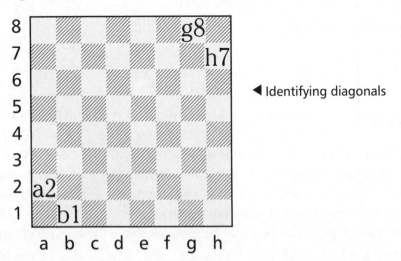

◀ Identifying diagonals

Size

Thus you can see a very important property of diagonals: They are not even close to being equal. Diagonals are made up of anywhere from two to eight squares. There are four diagonals containing two, three, four, five, six, and seven squares (two dark and two light), while there are two long diagonals, which each contain eight squares (one dark and one light).

The most important property of diagonals is that they are all made up of squares of one color. Diagonals are checkers' highways! There can never be a dark square on a light-square diagonal. Thus diagonals are limited-access highways compared to ranks and files.

Highways

So far we have learned about four types of roads on the chessboard. If you seem to remember only three, that's because you are not distinguishing between dark-square and light-square diagonals.

Any other highways are mostly ephemeral. Thus you can visualize the highway a1-a2-a3-a4-b5-c6-d7-e8. Since all squares border, it is definitely a highway. There are several pieces that could indeed travel that route. But it's actually nothing more than a mixture of the a-file and the a4-e8 diagonal.

Rectangular Corner

There is just one other type of highway that you need to know about. Because it doesn't involve bordering squares at all, it's questionable whether it can even be called a highway. It also has no name. So we will call it rectangular corner, since that describes the road (or obstacle course): Visualize a six-square rectangle anywhere on the chessboard. Now visualize opposite corners of that rectangle. That's the rectangular corner road, or course. It is bumpy, perhaps, but it's one you will get to know well.

Five Highways

The five types of chessboard highways are:

- Ranks
- Files
- Dark-square diagonals
- Light-square diagonals
- Rectangular corners

Squares

All the squares on a chessboard are not created equal, any more than any of the various types of highways are. To begin with, half of them are light and half of them are dark. Of course there is no essential difference between the dark and light squares.

The real difference between the various squares comes with their neighbors. How many squares does a particular square have bordering it? That's what makes some squares more equal than others.

Lots of Neighbors

Those squares that have many bordering squares are in the middle of a metropolis. There are pieces to see, squares to go to, and activity can be expected to be high. This is simply because there are many different directions that radiate out from such squares.

ALERT!

The geometrical center of the board (e4, d4, e5, d5) is where the most traffic will take place. The "greater center" of squares, encompassing c3-c6-f6-f3 and back to c3 and the center squares, usually encounters the next busiest activity. This is because these squares lead directly and quickly to anywhere.

For example, take a look at e4. There is the fourth rank, the e-file, and the b1-h7 and h1-a8 diagonals. In addition, the rectangular corners available from e4 are f6, g5, g3, f2, d2, c3, c5, and d6. Count up all the squares on major highways directly available from e4 and you will come up with an astounding thirty-five squares, or more than half the chessboard!

The Edge of the Board

On the other hand, take a look at the edge of the board. Anywhere along the a-file, the h-file, or the first or eighth rank will do. These squares all have some neighbors, but not nearly as many as those in our booming metropolis.

Let's do the same exercise with a corner square a1 that we did with the central square e4. From a1, we are directly connected with the a-file, the first rank, the a1-h8 diagonal, and the rectangular corners b3 and c2. That adds up to a paltry total of twenty-three.

Is it any wonder that one of the most important strategic principles in chess is to control the central squares? Ⓔ

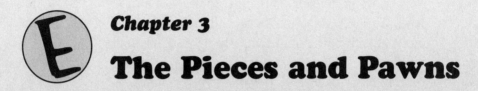

Chapter 3

The Pieces and Pawns

In checkers, there are two types of pieces: checkers and kings. So chess is quite a bit more complex, since there are six types of chessmen. This complexity at the very core of the game is what gives chess its great charm.

To Begin

All games of chess begin with White making a move. In reply, Black makes a move, and then it's White's turn again. The players continue alternating moves until one of a number of situations occur that ends the game. These situations are explored in detail in Chapter 4.

A move in chess is generally defined as a move by White and Black's reply. A single move by either White or Black with no reply is often called a half-move, or a "ply" in computer-talk.

FACT

On a computer screen or in a book or magazine, the board is almost always set up so that the White pieces are on the bottom and the Black pieces are at the top. There is no particular reason for this other than tradition. You could just as easily have the Black pieces at the bottom and the White pieces at the top.

The White pieces are set up along the first rank. The rooks begin at the outside corners, with the knights inside, the bishops next, and the king and queen in the middle. The White pawns line up on the second rank. The Black pieces begin on the eighth rank, and the Black pawns begin on the seventh rank. Kings are opposite each other on the e-file and queens are opposite each other on the d-file.

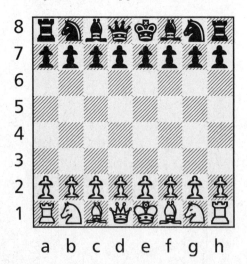

◀ Setting up a chessboard

Kings start out on the e-file. Just remember King Edward, and you'll never forget. The queens start out on the d-file. Queen Dolores will do. Also, remember that the queen takes her own color: The White queen starts out on d1, a light square, while the Black queen begins on d8, a dark square.

The King

Although there are six types of chessmen, the game of chess is really about the king. All other pieces and pawns are there as the king's helpers or weapons. The twin objectives of a chess game are to trap the opposing king and to keep your own king free. You will learn more about these objectives in Chapter 4. This twin objective is probably what makes chess unique. Most other games are measured in accumulations of points or time or territory.

Chess pieces have been designed to look like all kinds of things. This is fine for collections and displays. But for practical play, a design is needed that is at once easily recognizable by anyone who plays and readily available. That is the Staunton design, named after its inventor, nineteenth-century Shakespearean scholar and chess master, Englishman Howard Staunton.

Possible Moves

The chess king is not particularly strong or fast. He can move in any direction, along a rank, file, or diagonal, one square at a time. This may not sound very promising, but your monarch can have a lot of power late in the game when there are not too many other pieces around. He can have up to eight possible moves in the middle of the board, but only three possible moves from any corner.

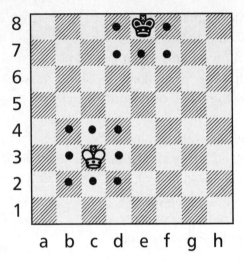

◀ The Black king can move to any of the five nearby dotted squares. The White king can move to any of the eight nearby dotted squares.

But the king is extremely valuable: get him trapped and you lose the game. Therefore good players often begin by hiding their big guy in an inaccessible corner, while attacking with their other pieces and pawns.

Captures

Although the king never leaves the board during a chess game, the king can capture other pieces. As long as the enemy piece is within range of the king (that means one square in any direction from where the king stands), he has the option of moving to the square occupied by the enemy piece and removing it from the board.

FACT

The pieces can be made of almost any material—wood and plastic are most common. Some chess pieces are virtual: they appear only on your computer screen. So long as there are sixteen White and sixteen Black pieces and pawns of the correct type, you have a viable set.

The Rook

This piece that looks like a tower is often incorrectly referred to as a *castle* by the uninitiated. But by any name, it is a powerful piece to have in your army, and a formidable enemy piece.

The rook moves along empty ranks or files. Place it on a1 on an empty board and it has fourteen possible moves, anywhere along the a-file or the first rank. Place it on e4 and it can go in four different directions: left along the fourth rank, right along the fourth rank, up (toward your opponent) along the e-file, or down (toward you) along the e-file.

The many possible squares the rook can move to give it a particularly rapid striking capacity. It is indeed a very similar piece to the chariot it was derived from. The rook started out as a chariot or a boat. It became a tower on a siege-engine during the Middle Ages. The word *rook* is not an English word translating any of these concepts, though. Instead, it is a mispronunciation of an old Sanskrit word for chariot.

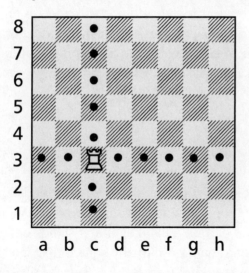

◀ The rook can move to any of the fourteen dotted squares. Rooks are powerful on an empty board.

Captures

The rook can capture any enemy piece (except the king) or pawn in its path. And although it is not possible to capture a king, if the enemy monarch should happen to be in the path of your rook, your opponent must drop everything else and remove the danger one way or another.

A capture is carried out by moving the rook along the rank or file desired to the square where the enemy piece or pawn resides. Place your rook on that square and remove the enemy piece or pawn from the board.

Long Range

Since the rook can swoop down the entire length or width of the board, it is referred to as a *long-range piece*. But this long-range capability is only good for rooks on an open board—that is, a board without a whole lot of obstacles in the way.

At the start of the game, the rooks are sleeping. None of them have any possible moves, so their power is only a potential for later use. Without open files or ranks the rook is pretty useless, and can get in the way of the other pieces.

Open files are files that are free of pawns. Other pieces, both enemy and friendly, can be on the file, and it is still open as long as no pawns reside there. Half-open files are files with an enemy pawn on it. Again, pieces of either color can clutter it up, as long as no friendly pawn is in the way.

The Bishop

The tall thin piece starting out between the royal couple and the knight is an expanded version of the old *alfil*, or "elephant." The bishop is another of the long-range pieces, and it operates on diagonals. So the bishop varies in strength depending in part on what diagonal it stands on.

A bishop on an empty board can move to any square diagonally forward or backward to either side of the square it stands on. If a piece or pawn stands in the way, however, that's where the bishop must stop. Bishops never learned how to jump.

Square Color

At the start of a chess game both opponents get two bishops: one dark-square bishop, which is confined to only dark squares for the duration of the game, and one light-square bishop, which is limited to the light squares only. Thus if your light-square bishop gets captured, you might conceivably become weak on the light squares. On the other hand, one of the best ways to begin an attack on the dark squares is to remove your opponent's dark-square bishop.

The bishop was originally an elephant in the Indian version of chess. It didn't get its modern powers until around the time of the Renaissance. The piece used to be a symbol of the elephant's tusks, and that symbol reminded the Italians of a bishop's miter.

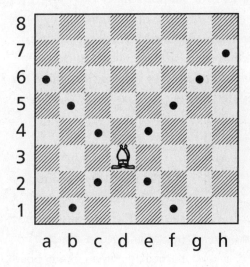

◀ The bishop can move to any of the eleven dotted squares. Bishops can be powerful on an empty board.

Captures

The bishop can capture any piece (except the king) or pawn located on any of its diagonals, provided nothing else is in the way. Simply move the bishop along the desired diagonal, stop at the square the enemy piece or pawn occupies, and remove the offender from the board.

The Queen

The other half of your royal couple is the superpiece of chess. Each side gets only one to begin with, and that's just as well—two would be awfully hard to deal with.

The queen is not only the most powerful chess piece; she is also the newest. The early Indian and Persian forms of chess had no queen. Instead, they gave the raja or shah a "viser," or counselor, that had approximately half the power of the monarch, and had to stay nearby. The new powerful queen is an invention of the Renaissance.

The queen is essentially a rook/bishop combination. She is another long-range piece, like the rook and the bishop, but she combines the power of both. Queens can operate on an empty board along ranks or files, just like a rook, and also along diagonals, just like a bishop. Furthermore, she can operate like both bishops, since in between diagonal moves, she can move along a file or rank and change the color of her diagonal. This is formidable power.

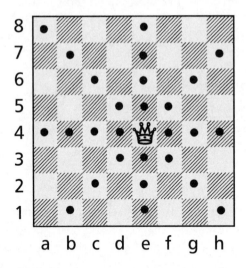

◄ The queen can move to any of the twenty-seven dotted squares. The queen is the most powerful piece in chess, particularly on an empty board.

Captures

The queen can capture just like any chess piece. Sight along rank, file, or diagonal from where your queen stands, find the piece or pawn you want to capture, and move the queen there, removing the enemy from the board. Provided nothing is in the way except empty squares, you have made a capture.

Tips on Use

The queen is so powerful that most beginning chess players want to bring her out right away to wreak havoc on the enemy position. But this is often a foolish strategy, since the very power of the queen can be turned against her. Any lesser piece or pawn (and in terms of power, that's all of them by definition) can come out and threaten to capture your powerful queen. She will wind up running from one attacker after another while your opponent pours more and more lesser pieces into the fight. It's generally better to hold off on bringing the queen into the attack until the way has been cleared. Then her true power can be unleashed.

The Knight

The peculiar child of chess, knights are shaped like a horse's head and don't behave like any of the other pieces. They do not move along ranks, files, or diagonals, either short-range like the king or long-range like the rook, bishop, or queen. Instead, the knight moves from one corner of any six-square rectangle to the opposite corner. Thus, the rectangular corner highway is what he uses. You will notice very quickly that a knight always winds up on a different color square from where he began his move. Thus in a way he is the bishop's opposite.

Knights are the cavalry of chess. Although there are no men or horses involved, the jumping action of the rectangular corner leap is close enough to have given players that impression. Along with the king, rook, and pawn, the knight represents one of the original pieces of the earliest Indian and Persian version of chess.

Other Explanations

The move of the knight is so strange that it takes some getting used to. It also allows for a wide variety of explanations. Many chess books introduce it as a piece that moves in an L-shape: one square forward along a file, then two squares at a ninety-degree angle along a rank; or two squares to the left along a rank, then one square backward along a file, etc.

But this L-shape puts emphasis on a square (along the bend) that has absolutely nothing to do with the knight's move.

Place a White knight in the center of the board; let's say on d5. Look at all the rectangles that use d5 as one of their corners. Now place a Black pawn on all the opposite corners. You should wind up with a Black pawn on c7, e7, f6, f4, e3, c3, b4, and b6. That is the knight's wheel, which is a great visualizing tool.

Another way of visualizing the knight's move is to think of this piece as a jumper. And as soon as you start to use the knight during a game where many other pieces are in the way, you will see that this is very true. Regardless of whether the squares in the middle of the rectangle are empty or occupied by friendly or enemy pieces, the knight can still make the jump.

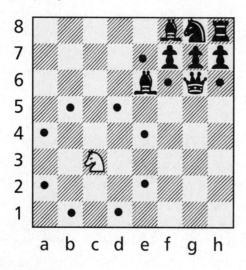

◀ The Black knight can move to any of the three dotted dark squares. The White knight can move to any of the eight dotted light squares.

Captures

Like the other pieces, the knight captures the same way it moves. Spring out from the square the knight occupies, and choose the occupied rectangular corner that is your destination. Land the knight on that square, removing the enemy from the board. You have just completed a knight capture.

ALERT!

> There are two different types of chessmen: the pieces and the pawns. The pieces include the king, rook, bishop, queen, and knight. They all capture the way they move and can operate in any direction. The pawns are very different creatures.

Types of Pieces

The five types of pieces can be divided up in several ways. One way is by function:

- King—The most important piece in the game
- Queen, rook, bishop, and knight—Helpers

Another way is by types of move the pieces are capable of. In which case, there are:

- Queen, rook, and bishop—Long-range
- King and knight—Short-range

Another way to divide up the pieces is by their strength:

- Major pieces—Queen and rook
- Minor pieces—Bishop and knight

You'll notice that the bishop is both a long-range and a minor piece. The reason is that, although its immediate power can be overwhelming, it can handle only half the squares on the chessboard during the life of any game.

The Pawns

These little peasants or foot soldiers are the plodders of chess. They move slowly, one square at a time, and only forward, never backward. In addition, they have many exceptions to the way they move, making them the toughest guys to master, despite their admitted weakness. It hardly seems worthwhile to put the time and effort into learning the moves!

FACT

The colors of the pieces can be whatever you like as long as they offer good contrast between the White and Black pieces. They don't actually have to be white and black; beige and red or cedar and maple are two possibilities.

But the pawn also represents upward mobility and democracy. Americans could well have invented it if it wasn't already in use by the time the New World was discovered. The pawn is everyman, and each one has a chance to make a difference in the game, if only he survives long enough.

Basic Move

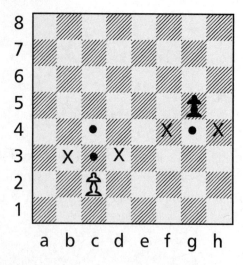

◄ The pawns can move to the nearby dotted squares or capture any piece or pawn standing on the nearby X squares.

The pawn's basic move is simple enough. Each pawn (each player starts out with eight of them) has the ability to move forward one square along a file or to capture one square forward along a diagonal. The capture is carried out by moving the pawn from its current square to one diagonally forward one square, removing the enemy piece or pawn there, and taking its place on that square. Right there we have a break from the pattern of the pieces, which move and capture in the same way.

Initial Two-Square Advance

The first time a pawn is used in a game he can move one square forward, as usual, or he can move two squares forward. Thereafter, the option is gone, whether or not it was used. Each pawn has this option whenever he is first moved, regardless of how many moves the game has gone.

Since the pawn moves forward on a file in this optional move, no capture is possible. The two-square-forward-along-a-file option is thus there to speed up play, nothing more. (The other exceptions, promotion and en passant, are explained in Chapter 5.) Ⓔ

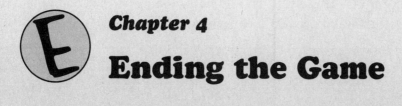

Chapter 4

Ending the Game

Now that you know how a game is played and the basic moves of the various pieces and pawns, it's time to learn how to get at what we are aiming for. And that, of course, is the king.

Check

The king is the whole game. Capturing the king, whether by accident or design, would end the game, perhaps prematurely. So the people who developed chess came up with a little insurance to make sure the game wouldn't end accidentally. Every time the king is threatened with capture, he is warned. This gives him a fighting chance to escape the fate of the other pieces and pawns. This warning is referred to as *check*.

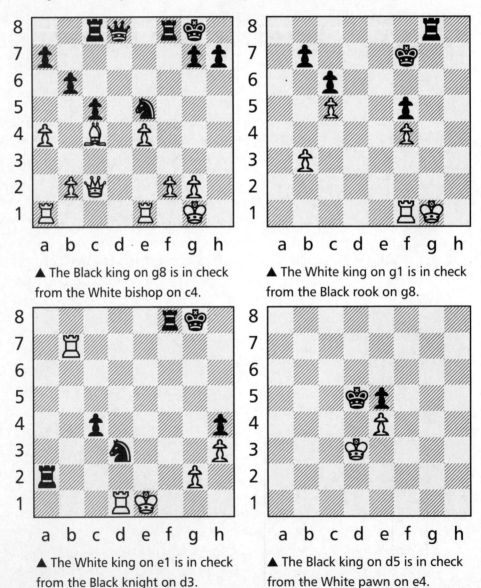

▲ The Black king on g8 is in check from the White bishop on c4.

▲ The White king on g1 is in check from the Black rook on g8.

▲ The White king on e1 is in check from the Black knight on d3.

▲ The Black king on d5 is in check from the White pawn on e4.

◀ The White king on a1 is in check from the Black queen on e5 along the a1–h8 diagonal.

A check is a situation where the king would be in danger of being captured if that were allowed. Instead, the player whose king is in check must drop everything and find a way to get out of check. Any piece or pawn is subject to a similar situation, but no warning is required and the player can ignore the threat to his piece or pawn if he wishes or if he is inattentive.

It sometimes happens that neither player noticed a check for several moves. When this is discovered, the players are required to retrace the moves until the king was first in check. It also sometimes happens (in the games of very inexperienced players) that both kings are in check. Such a situation is of course not allowed and the moves must be retraced to a point where only one king is in check.

Three Ways Out of Check

When your king is in check, you must find a way out. There are only three possible ways to get out of check. They are:

1. Capture the attacker.
2. Move the king.
3. Block the attack.

The first way is often the best way. By capturing the piece or pawn delivering the check you not only get out of check so the game can continue, you also remove something valuable to your opponent from the board. Killing two birds with one stone is always good strategy in a game you are trying to win.

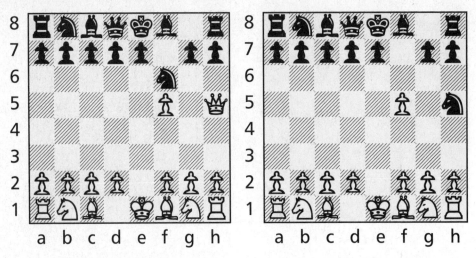

▲ The Black king on e8 is in check from the White queen on h5. Get out of check by capturing the queen with the knight on f6.

▲ Black has successfully gotten out of check, picking up a queen in the process.

The second way is the first thing inexperienced players think of, often the only thing. The king is in danger? Move him out of the way. But you must be careful to move the king to a safe square.

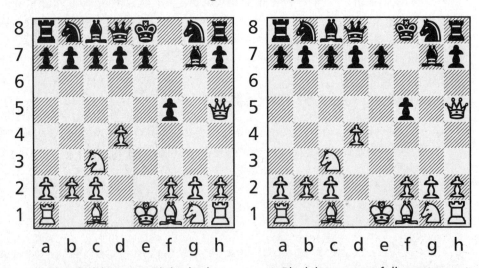

▲ The Black king on e8 is in check from the White queen on h5. Move the king to the safe square f8.

▲ Black has successfully gotten out of check by moving the king to a safe square.

The third way only works when your king is in check from a long-range piece with some squares in between the king and the attacking piece. You can block such a check by moving a friendly piece or pawn in the way of the attacker, thus cutting off its long-range power.

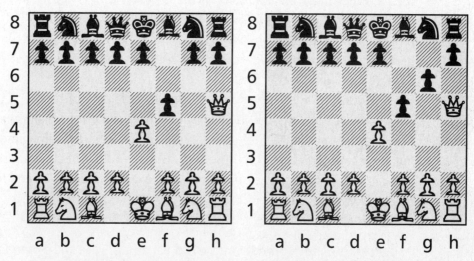

▲The Black king on e8 is in check from the White queen on h5. Block the check by moving the g-pawn to g6.

▲ Black has successfully gotten out of check by blocking the dangerous e8-h5 diagonal with the g-pawn. Note that the g-pawn is now ready to capture the queen in the next move.

Saying Check

When you place your opponent's king in check, you can say check if you wish, but this is not required. If your opponent is experienced, she will know that her king is in check and will go about trying to find a way out. The check itself is the warning. It is automatic and inherent in each check. Actually saying "check" is a reminder and that reminder is not required.

If your opponent is not very experienced, he may play a move that does not get his king out of check, thus forcing him to take the illegal move back and make another move that does get him out of check.

Checkmate

Just because you have three possible ways to get out of check doesn't mean one of them will always be available. Sometimes only two of the possible ways might be available, or maybe even only one of the ways will be available in a particular position. But what happens if none of the possible solutions happens to present itself? What if you can't get out of check? Then the game is over. Your king is trapped and you lose. This situation is known as *checkmate*.

Checkmate is a position where a king is in check and there is no saving move. Capturing the checking piece or pawn either is not possible or such a capture would leave the king in check anyway. Anywhere the king moves will still leave him in check. Blocking the check is either impossible or blocking one check will still leave the king in check from another direction.

FACT

Checkmate may come from the old Persian phrase *shah manad*, meaning "the king is helpless." Some think it comes from *shah mat*, meaning "the king is dead," but how can that be? The king never dies in chess; he is trapped in a checkmate, not killed. That is perhaps the chief unique identifier of chess.

It is not as easy to checkmate a king as it is to capture something else. It isn't enough to simply threaten the king; you also have to make sure there are no ways out.

Since checkmate is our objective in a game of chess, it's a good idea to know what it looks like. So here are a few diagrams with checkmates depicted.

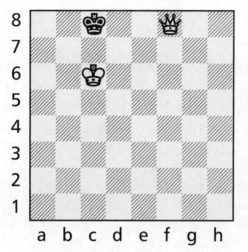

▲ The Black king is checkmated. He is in check from the queen on f8 along the eighth rank and cannot escape to the seventh rank since the White king controls those squares.

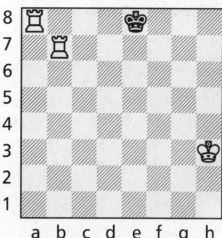

▲ The Black king is checkmated. He is in check from the rook on a8 along the eighth rank and cannot escape to the seventh rank since the White rook on b7 controls those squares.

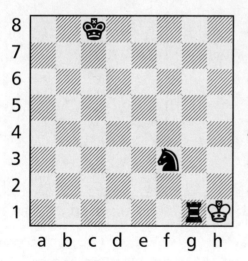

▲ The White king is checkmated. The rook controls h1 and g2, while the knight controls the g1 and h2 escape squares.

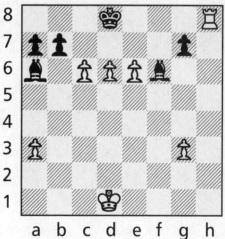

▲ The Black king is checkmated. The rook controls the entire eighth rank, while the pawns control the seventh rank escape squares.

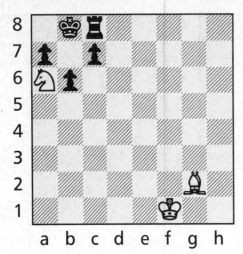

▲ The Black king is checkmated. The knight delivers the check, while the bishop controls the diagonal escape squares.

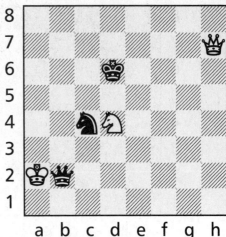

▲ The White king is checkmated. The Black queen checks and controls all the escape squares except her own b2, which is controlled by the c4-knight.

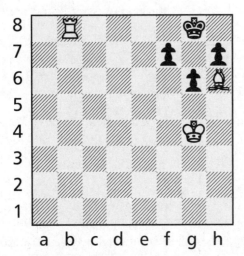

▲ The Black king is checkmated. The rook delivers the check and covers eighth rank escape squares, while the bishop controls g7.

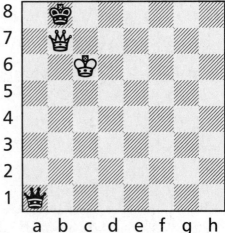

▲ The Black king is checkmated. The White queen checks and controls all the escape squares except her own b7, which is controlled by the White king.

▲ The White king is checkmated. The knight delivers the check while the rook controls the second rank escape squares.

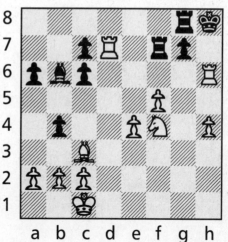

▲ The Black king is checkmated. The h6-rook delivers the check and controls escape squares. Meanwhile, the g7-pawn cannot capture since that would expose the king to check from the c3-bishop.

Winning and Losing

Although checkmate is the goal of a chess game, it is not the only way to end every game. There are at least three other ways to win or lose a game:

- You can win when your opponent runs out of time.
- You can win when your opponent resigns, giving you the game.
- You can win when your opponent fails to show up for a scheduled game, thus forfeiting.

Winning Without Checkmate

In order to run your opponent out of time you have to be using chess clocks. You will learn about chess clocks in the next chapter.

The next way to win without checkmate is the most common of all. Most experienced players don't wait for checkmate. They can see it coming, often a long way off. So, rather than fight on in a hopeless situation, they will resign the game, which can be done by tipping over their king or offering to shake their opponent's hand or simply saying "I resign."

FACT

A great player once jumped up on the top of the table, threw his king across the room, and shouted "Why must I lose to this idiot?" This is not the recommended way of resigning, however. Nor is the unsportsmanlike trick of picking up and leaving the game while your clock is ticking, thus forcing your opponent to wait until your time runs out in order to record his win.

Finally, there is the dreaded forfeit. This is an unavoidable consequence of large tournaments; nevertheless, nobody likes them. The winner never got to play a game. The people he passed by with this unearned victory rather resent being beaten out in the standings by someone who didn't play all their games. And the tournament director has to explain it all and try to make this seeming nonsense make sense. But what else can you do when a player shows up for a game and her opponent doesn't show up? So the forfeit has a place in chess and is here to stay.

Nobody Wins or Loses

There is another way to end a chess game altogether. It is possible for a chess game to end in a draw or a tie, with neither player winning or losing.

In a formal tournament or match, each game is recorded as 1 point for the winner and 0 points for the loser. If the game is a draw, the game is recorded as ½ a point for each player. Thus two draws are equivalent to a win and a loss in a tournament or a match.

There are various ways to "split the point" (draw or tie) in a chess game. They range from the opponents simply agreeing to end hostilities to various ways provided for in the rules of chess that cover situations where one player may have an advantage, but cannot or will not push that advantage through to a checkmate. These situations are described below in detail.

Draw by Agreement

The simplest form of draw is the one by agreement. One player offers a draw to his opponent and that player agrees. Anyone can offer a draw at any time during a game, but it is considered bad manners and unsportsmanlike conduct to offer repeatedly after being turned down. It is also considered good etiquette to offer a draw on your own time. Naturally, this applies only to timed games.

When offered a draw it is considered courteous to at least acknowledge the offer. You might say "I'll think about it" if you're not ready with an immediate "No!" or "You got it!"

Stalemate

This draw is a strange situation. It is a mate and ends the game, but there is no check. In a stalemate, there is nothing one of the players can do. Although her king is not in check, any move she makes will expose her king to check, and that is not allowed. So we know that a stalemate ends the game.

QUESTION?

Why is stalemate a draw?
The quick answer is because the rules say it is. There is really no logic behind it, and at various times in the past, stalemate counted as a win for the stronger side or even a win for the weaker side! The only thing sure about a stalemate is that the game cannot continue, since it is against the rules to place your king in check.

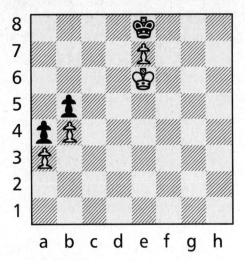

◄ With Black to move, the game ends in stalemate. Black has no legal moves available, and is not in check.

In some stalemates, one player may have an enormous advantage. He may have many pieces and pawns left while his opponent is left with a lone king. Yet, since that king has no moves, the game ends and is declared a draw.

◄ With White to move, the game ends in stalemate. Somehow Black went terribly wrong to get this far ahead and not win.

It is a situation that may seem unfair, but that's only if you are the one left with the large advantage. Perhaps with such a large advantage you could have found a way to herd the lone king into a corner and checkmate him. Thus, allowing a player with a lone king to escape with a stalemate is often nothing more than carelessness.

On the other hand, if you are the one with the lone king, you might see stalemate as a fantastic opportunity. There have been combinations (see Chapter 10) played where a competitor, sensing trouble, got rid of his remaining pieces in order to bring about a stalemate to end the game in a draw. These types of combinations are available to those who look for them.

So don't disdain stalemate; use it as a weapon. After all, ½ a point is better than none.

Insufficient Mating Material

Here's a case of a well-thought-out rule. Since nobody can produce a checkmate even if both players cooperate in the demise of one, the game is automatically called a *draw*.

Easy Cases

The simplest case is king against king. Next simplest is king and minor piece against king. These situations are automatic, because the players could play moves until the cows come home and nobody could ever produce a checkmate. Notice that positions with pawns do not qualify. Pawns can promote, as you will learn in Chapter 5, so there is always sufficient mating material as long as a single pawn is on the board.

Not So Easy

When we get to king and minor piece against king and minor piece, however, we start getting into some trouble. A king and knight cannot checkmate another king and knight, and a king and bishop cannot checkmate another king with a same-colored bishop. But a king and bishop can checkmate a king and knight or a king with an opposite-colored bishop. And a king and knight can checkmate a king and bishop.

All these positions are rather obscure, however. Although checkmates are possible in such positions, they cannot be forced. These checkmates require a cooperative opponent. So for all practical purposes, all such positions are generally abandoned as drawn.

ALERT!

A king and two knights cannot force a lone king into submission. Incredible but true. It takes a rook or queen or two bishops or a bishop and a knight to force a checkmate on a lone king. Or a lonely pawn, who can promote into a rook or queen and thus create enough checkmating material.

Three-Position Repetition

This one is not always completely understood, even by very experienced players. That is because the rule is a bit dry and players have memorized it in a slightly edited form.

The Rule

This rule is actually called *Triple occurrence of position* in the *Official Rules of Chess*. It runs:

> *The game is drawn upon a claim by a player on the move when the same position is about to appear for at least the third time or has just appeared for at least the third time, the same player being on move each time. In both cases, the position is considered the same if pieces of the same kind and color occupy the same squares and if the possible moves of all the pieces are the same, including the right to castle or to capture a pawn en passant.*

Position, Not Moves

Most players think of this rule as repeating the same move three times consecutively. But you will notice that there is no mention of repeating moves or the same position occurring consecutively.

Most often this draw will come about by the players repeating moves in order, since that is the easiest way to bring about a repetition of the same position. But it is possible to throw in other moves or to repeat the same position with a different move order, so it's a good idea to know the rule as it is stated in the rule book.

Here is an example of this triple occurrence of position draw:

▲ White is in trouble, but the Black king is exposed. So White begins to check. The White queen moves to b8 to check. The Black king moves to g7, and the White queen moves to e5 to check again.

▲ The Black king has to go back to the eighth rank, but he wants to avoid moving to f8, because then the White queen can move to h8 for checkmate. The Black king moves to g8. The White queen then moves to b8 for check. Note that this is the second time this position has occurred.

The Black king then moves to g7. The White queen checks at e5. The Black king escapes to g8 and the White queen again moves to b8 for check.

The intention of the triple occurrence of position draw is that the players are only wasting time if they keep coming back to the same position. The player who is trying to win must somehow come up with some sort of progress toward a checkmate, while the player who is trying to draw merely has to keep repeating the position.

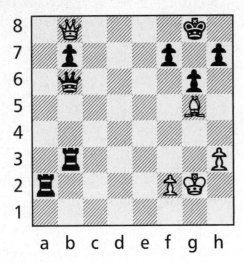

◄ You no doubt recognize this position by now. It is the third time it has occurred, and the game is therefore drawn.

Fifty-Move Rule

This rule also is intended to prevent players from wasting time by playing random moves that lead nowhere. Under the fifty-move rule, if no pawns are moved and no captures are made in fifty consecutive moves, the game is declared a draw. Fifty moves in this rule is defined as fifty moves by White and fifty moves by Black, so that is still a lot of moves.

Throughout the 1990s there was a push to expand the fifty-move rule to a seventy-five-move rule or a hundred-move rule. This was to accommodate certain positions where computer programs found ways to force checkmate that required more than fifty moves of maneuvering without moving a nonexistent pawn or making a capture. Positions such as king, rook, and bishop against king and rook are susceptible to this extension of the fifty-move rule. There is as yet no consensus on whether or not these rule changes should be made universal. Sometimes the changed rules are in effect, and other times the old fifty-move rule is in effect. A tournament director should therefore make clear which rules are in effect for his event.

In a way this is a very exciting time to be a chess player. It has been hundreds of years since the last big changes in the rules began. Today, thanks to the influence of computers, it is possible we may be seeing another set of rule changes. Ⓔ

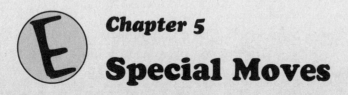

Chapter 5

Special Moves

Y ou now know how a chess game is conducted, at least in general, and the basic moves of the pieces and pawns. So what's next? Why, all those pesky exceptions to the rules known as *special moves*. There are quite a few, so let's begin.

Touch Move

The first special move isn't an exception at all. In fact, it should never be an exception, despite the take-back feature on many of today's chess-playing computers. It is the notorious touch-move rule.

The Rule

The rule is simple enough: If you touch a piece or pawn, you should then move that piece or pawn. If you have made a move and let go of whatever piece or pawn you moved, your move is completed.

This rule is sensible and fair. And it is often abused in casual chess. Many players, particularly those who are not very experienced, will notice that something is wrong about a move in the process of making that move or just after making it. Then the temptation to change the move is often hard to resist.

But it is simply bad manners to change the move in the process of making it, and even poorer manners to change a move that has already been made. Besides, changing the rule is against the rules of chess, as well as against the rules of good sportsmanship.

J'adoube

There are many foreign terms interspersed throughout chess, just like there are foreign terms in music and science—well, maybe not so many as in science. One of these terms is the French expression *j'adoube*, which means "I adjust." It refers to handling the pieces or pawns prior to making a move when you have no intention of making a move. You may want to do this to adjust the pieces so that they are neater, setting in the center of the squares, or you may simply want to pick up a piece that has fallen down and place it on its proper square.

QUESTION?

Should I say *j'adoube* if I accidentally touch a piece?
Yes, and immediately, if not sooner. If your opponent doesn't hear *j'adoube* or "I adjust," how can she know the touch was accidental?

However, how can your opponent know your intention? If he sees you touch your queen, and he knows that he will win if you move your queen, he may be highly motivated to claim the touch-move rule. But you can circumvent that simply by saying *j'adoube* or "I adjust," the English equivalent. That way everybody knows you had no intention of moving your queen.

Promotion

The basic move of the pawn leaves a rather large hole, which I hope you at least wondered about. What happens when a pawn reaches the far side of the board and there is nowhere else to go? Since a pawn can't move sideways or backward, what use is it?

ALERT!

When you are ready to promote a pawn and there are no queens available, you can usually get a hold of a captured rook and turn it upside down. If none are available, you can place two pawns on the square or turn a piece or pawn on its side. There is always a way!

This is where promotion comes in. Any pawn, upon reaching the farthest possible rank (the eighth rank for White pawns and the first rank for Black pawns) undergoes a metamorphosis. You remove the pawn from the board and replace it with a piece.

Promotion, by the way, has nothing whatsoever to do with any of the pieces already on the board, or even with any of the pieces captured. A pawn upon promoting theoretically turns into whatever piece you want it to turn into.

Practically speaking, this doesn't happen, of course. Instead, you must search among captured pieces or get a hold of another set in order to make a second or third queen, for instance. If nothing is available, however, you'll find a way.

A New Queen

You always have a choice as to which piece you want to turn the pawn into. But first consider the restrictions: The pawn cannot remain a pawn, and it cannot become a king. Nor can it become an enemy piece (not that you'd even want to make it into one!).

This choice is most often not thought about at all. The queen is such a powerful piece that almost every pawn that is promoted is promoted into a queen. In fact, this is often called *queening* the pawn.

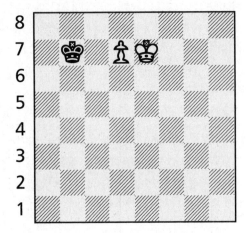

▲ White is poised to promote the pawn. Remember that White pawns move up the board, while Black pawns travel down the board.

▲ White has turned the little pawn into a queen. This is a rule that made it into Lewis Carroll's *Through the Looking Glass*.

Underpromotion

Nevertheless, there are times when you might not want a queen. In these cases, it's good to know that the choice is yours. You can promote to a rook, a bishop, or a knight, as well as a queen. As for why you might want to do such a ridiculous-seeming thing, a very simple example will suffice.

◀ White's pawn is ready to promote. Should it become a queen?

Look at the diagram. You are White and it is your move. If you promote the pawn to a queen your opponent will then checkmate you and you will lose. If, however, you underpromote the pawn to a knight, it is checkmate and you win!

◀ White has decided that greedily promoting to a queen and losing is not the way to go. Underpromotion to a knight produces this checkmate.

Just keep in mind that the choice is yours every time you promote a pawn, and the choice is your opponent's every time she promotes one of her pawns.

Promotion with a Capture

One of the most spectacular changes you can bring about during a chess game is to capture a piece, let's say the opponent's queen, with a pawn while promoting it to a queen. To gain two queens in one move is unbelievable, but it is actually possible.

▲ Black has a pawn for a queen. But it is Black's move, and Black pawns march downward.

▲ In one move Black has transformed her pawn into a queen while capturing the White queen.

En Passant

Another French term in general use with chess players is *en passant*. This means in passing, and it refers to a particular situation that comes up from time to time in games. It doesn't happen in more than one game in ten, perhaps, but it is a rule you should be aware of if you want to play chess or follow the games of others. To understand en passant, you have to go back to the rule about the pawn's initial two-square option on its first move.

The Situation

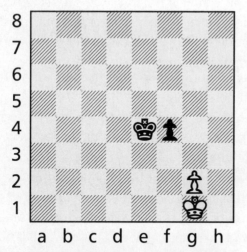

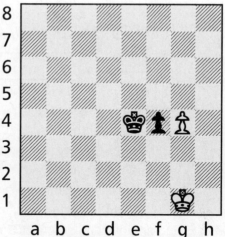

▲You are playing the White pieces and have a pawn on g2. You have the option of moving that pawn to g3 or g4. Your opponent has a pawn on f4.

▲ If you move your pawn to g3, your opponent might decide to capture your pawn with her pawn. Therefore, you decide to exercise you two-square-forward option and move your pawn to g4.

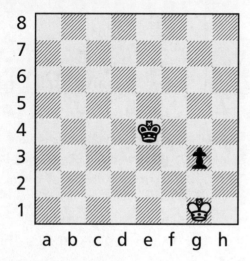

◄ But your opponent captures the pawn on g3, just as if you had moved it there!

This is perfectly legal, and it is a rule you simply have to know about. To repeat, the situation leading up to en passant is:

- A White pawn is on the second rank, unmoved (or a Black pawn is on the seventh rank, unmoved).
- A Black pawn is on an adjacent file on the fourth rank (or a White pawn is on an adjacent file on the fifth rank).
- White exercises the option to move the pawn two squares forward instead of one (or Black exercises the option to move the pawn two squares forward instead of one).
- The Black pawn that was on an adjacent file on the fourth rank captures the White pawn that has just moved two squares forward as if it had moved one square forward (or the White pawn that was on an adjacent file on the fifth rank captures the Black pawn that has just moved two squares forward as if it had moved one square forward).

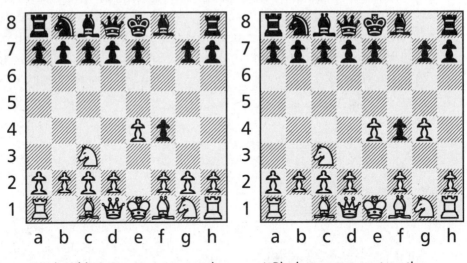

▲ It is White's turn to move, and White decides to move the g-pawn up two squares.

▲ Black can now capture the g4-pawn on g3. Notice that Black cannot capture the e4-pawn.

Without en passant, a pawn that has made its way into the opponent's territory would lose some of its power, and opposing pawns could pass by with impunity.

Restrictions

It is important to remember that an en passant capture can only take place under the specialized conditions just explained. A piece can never capture anything en passant, while a pawn can never capture a piece en passant. In addition, a pawn can never capture another pawn en passant unless that pawn has just exercised its two-squares-forward optional move.

A further restriction on en passant is that the capture has to be executed as a direct response to the two-square-forward move of the opposing pawn. Wait one move and you lose the option of capturing en passant.

For an example, let's go back to the position where White has that pawn on g2 while Black has the pawn on f4. Let's also say that White has a king on g1 while Black has a king on g8. White moves his pawn forward under to two-square-forward option to g4. Black responds by moving her king to g7. White then moves his king to g2. Now it is Black's turn, and there is no longer any option to capture the White pawn en passant.

Castling

Unlike en passant, this one comes up often. Practically every game one or the other of the players castles or has a chance to castle. Like en passant, castling is a very restricted move. Certain conditions have to be filled in order to be able to castle.

King and Rook

Before we get into the special conditions, the basic castling move consists of moving both a king and a rook on the same turn. It is the only time in chess when you can move two friendly pieces on the same turn. The king moves two squares along his home rank, while the rook jumps over the king and lands on the opposite side he started from. Both moves are impossible separately, since kings normally move only one square in any direction while rooks normally don't jump over anything, needing a clear file or rank in order to move at all.

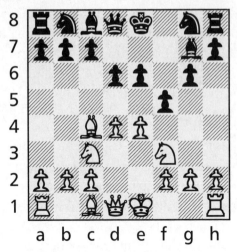

▲ White's king and h1-rook have not moved. There is nothing in between the two except empty squares.

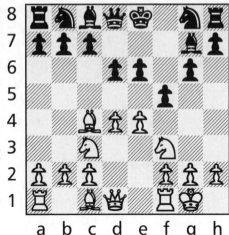

▲ White has moved the king two squares to the right along the first rank and jumped the rook over the king to its other side. Castling is completed.

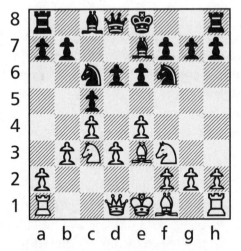

▲ Black's king and h8-rook have not moved. There is nothing in between the two except empty squares.

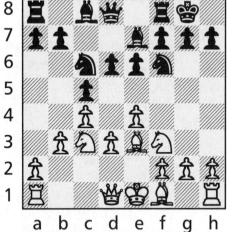

▲ Black has moved the king two squares to the right along the eighth rank and jumped the rook over the king to its other side. Castling is completed.

Castling serves two purposes. One is to tuck the vulnerable king away in a corner for safety during the early part of the game. Opposing pieces may be flying around the middle of the board, and staying there may not be healthy for the valuable king. The other is to allow the rook to get involved in the action through the middle of the board. This is usually much better than moving the rook up the h- or a-file along the edge of the board.

Conditions

In order for castling to be possible, the following conditions have to be present:

- The squares between king and rook must be empty.
- Both king and rook must be on their original square.
- Both king and rook must be unmoved.
- The king cannot castle into check.
- The king cannot castle out of check. Remember, the three ways out of check did not include castling.
- The king cannot castle through check.

FACT

Castling is the newest move in chess. It has been standardized only within the last 150 years. Before that there were many ways to castle, including the king and rook actually trading places or using it as two separate moves, with the king moving first and the rook jumping over him the next move.

That last restriction is a little tricky. It means that the king can't pass over any square that is directly under control of an enemy piece. For example, a White king on e1 and a White rook on h1 are ready to castle, as long as neither has moved and the king is not in check and the f1- and g1-squares are empty. But if there is a Black bishop on d3, which controls the f1-square, castling is not possible.

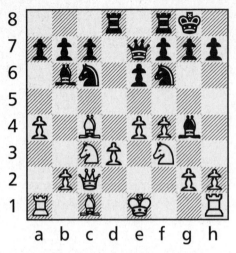

▲ White cannot castle because the king would wind up on g1, in check from the b6-bishop.

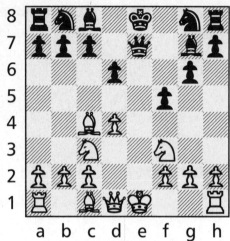

▲ White cannot castle because the king is in check from the Black queen along the e-file.

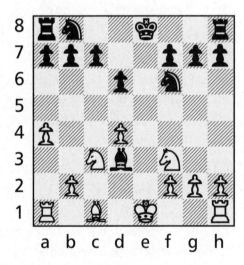

◄ White cannot castle because the f1-square he must pass over is controlled by the d3-bishop.

Kingside and Queenside

There are two types of castling, depending on which direction you decide to castle. In kingside castling the White king goes to g1 while the White h1-rook goes to f1. (The Black king goes to g8 while the Black h8-rook goes to f8.) The kingside is simply the half of the board where the kings start out. Thus kingside refers to the e-, f-, g-, and h-files.

In queenside castling, the king goes in the other direction. The queenside is that half of the board where the queens start out. Thus queenside refers to the d-, c-, b-, and a-files. The White king goes to c1 and the White rook on a1 goes to d1. (The Black king goes to c8 while the Black rook on a8 goes to d8.)

 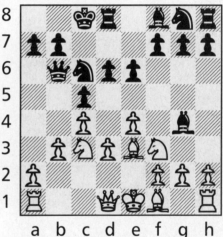

▲ Black's king and a8-rook have not moved. There is nothing in between the two except empty squares.

▲ Black has moved the king two squares to the left along the eighth rank and jumped the rook over the king to its other side. Queenside castling is completed.

The restrictions about castling out of, into, and through check apply only to the king. If your rook is under attack from an enemy piece but your king is safe on its starting square, the square it passes over in the process of castling, and the square it lands on, castling is legal.

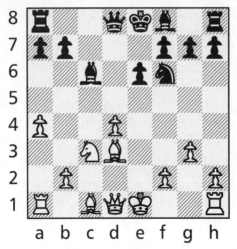

▲ White's king and rook have not moved and there is nothing but empty squares between the two.

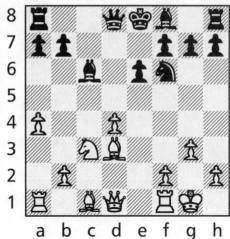

▲ White has completed castling. The rook was under attack, but that's not relevant to castling.

The enemy can also cover the extra square the rook passes over in queenside castling during castling.

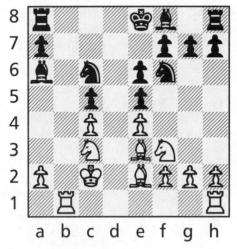

▲ The White rook covers the b8-square, but this is not relevant when castling comes into play.

▲ Black has successfully castled. The b8-square doesn't involve the king, so its situation is not relevant.

You will notice that in queenside castling there is an extra file to take into account. The king always moves two squares to the side when castling, so it is the rook that has to travel farther in queenside castling.

ALERT!

A particularly important restriction to castling is that it can only be played once in a game by either player. This is inherent in the castling rules, since castling cannot take place unless the king and the rook he castles with are unmoved. Thus once you castle, that condition can no longer be met for the rest of the game.

The Clock

We've covered all the special moves in chess as long as you don't consider the chess clock. But clocks are often used to time games, whether in tournaments or in clubs or just to make a game go fast in a friendly game in somebody's home, in a park, or on the Internet.

A chess clock is really two clocks in one housing. When you make a move, press the button on your clock and your clock will stop ticking while your opponent's clock will begin ticking. When your opponent makes his move, your clock will start ticking while his clock stops ticking. That way the entire game can be timed, with each player only being charged for the time it takes to come up with her move.

Chess clocks come in two types. A digital chess clock (sometimes referred to as *allegro*) is one that displays the exact number of minutes and seconds available for each player. When a player runs out of time using a digital clock, the display will read 00:00. A mechanical clock (sometimes referred to as *analog*) is one with the traditional clock face and hands. A mechanical clock also has a device called a *flag* that signals when a player's time has expired. When a player runs short of time using a mechanical clock, the hands of the clock will begin to raise the player's flag. When time expires, the player's flag falls.

Speed or Rapid Chess

Chess players often want to play a great number of games very quickly. There are various reasons for wanting to do this, but we'll just look at how to do it. For that you need a chess clock. You set the clock for five minutes for each player (or seven minutes, three minutes, or thirty minutes or whatever you want) and commence playing.

As long as the players remember to push in the button at the top of their side of the clock, the game will move along until someone plays a checkmate or gets one of various drawn positions. Or until somebody's flag falls. That person has run out of time and automatically loses, just as if he had been checkmated.

Bullet Play

A variation on speed play is the bullet chess so popular on the Internet. That usually allows one minute for the game by each player. Of course, you don't use a digital or a mechanical clock for such chess, since the clock is automatic, and your move triggers the change of time from you to your opponent and back again.

Slower Time Limits

Yet another way to use a chess clock is to give each player a set amount of time for a set amount of moves. A very popular time limit used to be forty moves in two hours. In this version of timed chess, the players must keep score of the game if they want to be able to make a claim that their opponent overstepped the time limit. Otherwise, how could anybody know that the forty moves were reached?

FACT

New rules have been made to accommodate players who are easily winning the position but have no time to play out the win. These include lack of mating material, insufficient losing chances, and a new device on chess clocks known as *time increments*. It's all there waiting for you if you should decide to get involved in tournament chess.

In a slower time limit, keeping track of the moves is an essential ingredient. You will learn more about keeping score of a game in the next chapter. Ⓔ

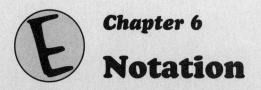

Chapter 6
Notation

Chess notation is probably as old as chess. It is nothing more than a way to record games and positions and problems and combinations so that they can be reproduced. Such notation provides a way to read and write chess, so a record can be kept of any chess game.

Why Keep Records?

There are many reasons for keeping a record of a chess game. Unless you have a fantastic memory, keeping score of a game is the best way to have the moves available for critique afterward. This is one of the best ways to improve your game, whether the critique is done by you alone, or you with your opponent (better), or you and your opponent along with a third party, perhaps an experienced player (best).

The Chess World

Knowing how to read a game score brings the entire world of chess into your home. There are newspaper columns, chess magazines, and a fantastically huge number of chess books on the market. Chess masters have been writing down their thoughts, analysis, and systems for hundreds of years. This is all open to one who knows how to read chess notation and opaque to one who does not know how.

Chess-playing computers, chess-playing software programs, huge chess databases, and chess Web pages all use chess notation. You're missing out on an awful lot if you don't know how to read chess.

If you ever decide that you want to improve at chess, you will need to know chess notation. Whether you want to get good enough to beat the computer or someone in particular or to gain a national or international title or rating, you simply cannot progress without it. No coach or teacher will be able to do much with you if you don't have game scores to work with, and you won't even be able to scrutinize your own games without this knowledge.

FACT

Blindfold chess, and especially simultaneous blindfold chess, can only be accomplished by those who understand chess notation. The chess master, who has no set or board in sight, calls out her moves. The opponent or opponents, who have sets and boards in front of them and can see the game in progress, call out their response.

Win on Time

You win if your opponent runs out of the allotted time before making the prescribed number of moves in a tournament game. The only way to show that this has indeed happened, though, is to have your game score ready along with the clock that shows the time is up. Obviously this cannot be done unless you have kept a record of the game.

Correspondence and e-mail chess are not possible without chess notation. For that matter, chess played over the telephone and blindfold chess are also prohibitively difficult without a notation system.

FACT

There have been more books written about chess than about all other games combined. The game has a wide appeal, and its language is understood all over the world. Knowing the language of chess can put you in touch with people from every corner of the globe.

You Already Know the Basics!

After having just learned how widespread chess is, would it be a surprise to learn that you already know the basics of chess notation? Well, prepare to be surprised, because you already do!

You already know what each square is called, after all, and you know the names of each and every rank and file and diagonal on the board. In addition, you already know the names of all the chess pieces and pawns and the names of their special moves. You also know about check, checkmate, and stalemate.

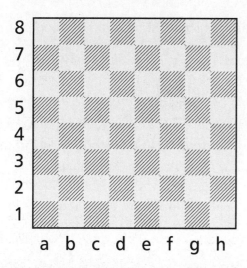

◄ The chessboard is accompanied by the letters of the files and the numbers of the ranks.

Battleship

Have you ever played Battleship? That's the game where you hide your ships on a grid and try to destroy the ships of your opponent on his grid by calling out coordinates. The grids aren't checkered, but the grid coordinates are none other than chess square coordinates: e1, g2, h4, a7, etc. All right, so there are a few other things to know about chess notation, but again, you are already familiar with everything here.

Recording Your Opinion

You can record your opinion about a move of a chess game very succinctly: Just use punctuation. The following table of punctuation marks that follow moves is understood all over the world. Whenever you see such punctuation after a move, you know that it is the opinion of the annotator (the one writing about the game).

Punctuation Mark	Meaning
!	A very good or surprising move
!!	A particularly strong and surprising move
?	A weak move
??	A blunder; giving something away
!?	An interesting move
?!	A dubious move that has some strong points

Specifics

Pieces are designated by capital letters: K is for king, Q is for queen, R is for rook, B is for bishop, and N is for knight (not K since that is reserved for the king). The pawn has no symbol. It used to be P, but that has been done away with in the interest of simplicity.

Moves are written as the piece symbol of the piece being moved and the square that piece lands on. Captures are indicated by an x between the piece symbol and the square the capture takes place on.

Check is indicated by a + after the move, and checkmate is indicated simply by writing checkmate after the move that produces it. Stalemate is handled in the same way.

Any ambiguities (such as when you have a rook on a1 and a rook on h1 and nothing in between and want to move one of your rooks to d1) are handled by simply adding an extra identifying letter or number. In the case just cited, Rad1 or Rhd1 will convey your meaning precisely.

Keep in mind that all square names and file symbols contain lowercase letters only. Capital letters are reserved for the piece symbols.

ALERT!

Castling is indicated in chess notation by the use of zeros to indicate the number of squares between the king and rook separated by a hyphen. Thus castling kingside looks like 0-0, while castling queenside looks like 0-0-0.

Move Numbers

The moves are all numbered, beginning with the first move, which is move one, and the next move, which is move two, etc. Since White moves first, his move is given first. Next you give Black's move. You just have to remember that Black's first move is part of move one.

Pawn Moves

Just like the movement of the pawn, the notation for pawn moves is different. When a pawn moves, it is written simply as the destination square. You would expect a typical first move to be written 1. Pe4, but actually it is the simpler 1. e4. When pawns capture, the notation is the file letter followed by the x for a capture followed by the destination square (4. dxe5). When a pawn promotes, it is written as the move followed by an equal sign followed by the symbol for the piece the pawn has promoted to (d8=Q or hxg8=N+).

An entire game can thus be described in a single paragraph. Get out a chessboard and set up the pieces for the start of a game and play through the following game.

1. e4 e5 2. Nf3 d6 3. d4 Bg4 4. dxe5 Bxf3 5. Qxf3 dxe5 6. Bc4 Nf6 7. Qb3 Qe7 8. Nc3 c6 9. Bg5 b5 10. Nxb5 cxb5 11. Bxb5+ Nbd7 12. 0-0-0 Rd8 13. Rxd7 Rxd7 14. Rd1 Qe6 15. Bxd7+ Nxd7 16. Qb8+ Nxb8 17. Rd8 checkmate.

◄ This is the final position. If you have come up with something else, go back and make sure you play all the moves correctly.

Algebraic Notation

What you have just read through is a game written in algebraic notation. Change the piece symbols to small pictures of the pieces and you have an international language, understood by chess players everywhere. This form of algebraic notation is called *figurine algebraic*.

White: Paul Morphy
Black: Duke and Count
Paris, 1858
1. e4 e5 2. ♘f3 d6 3. d4 ♗g4 4. dxe5 ♗xf3 5. ♕xf3 dxe5 6. ♗c4 ♘f6 7. ♕b3 ♕e7 8. ♘c3 c6 9. ♗g5 b5 10. ♘xb5 cxb5 11. ♗xb5+ ♘bd7 12. 0-0-0 ♖d8 13. ♖xd7 ♖xd7 14. ♖d1 ♕e6 15. ♗xd7+ ♘xd7 16. ♕b8+ ♘xb8 17. ♖d8 checkmate.

▲ The game you have just played through is presented in figurine algebraic notation.

Long and Short Forms

There are other forms of algebraic notation besides the forms you have just learned about. There is long form, where the square the piece or pawn comes from is recorded as well as the square it goes to, like this: 1. e2-e4 e7-e5 2. Ng1-f3 d7-d6 3. d2-d4 Bc8-g4 4. d4xe5 Bg4xf3, etc. Then there is short form, which dispenses with anything unnecessary. Even the capture sign is done away with, since playing over the game makes the capture obligatory anyway: 1. e4 e5 2. Nf3 d6 3. d4 Bg4 4. de Bf3, etc.

English Descriptive Notation

In the old English descriptive notation the files are given the names of the pieces which occupy the first square on them in the original position. To distinguish the two sides of the board from one another (right vs. left), those pieces near the king are known as KR (king's rook), KN (king's knight), and KB (king's bishop). Similarly, those nearest the queen are known as QR (queen's rook), QN (queen's knight), and QB (queen's bishop).

FACT

Descriptive notation used to be popular in many countries, but it is more complex than algebraic notation and isn't universal. Many of the old classic chess books written in descriptive notation have since been translated into algebraic notation.

The eight files with their descriptions are identical for White and Black. The ranks are numbered from one to eight, with each player beginning from his or her own side, so that "1" for White is "8" for Black. In this way, each square carries a unique letter and a number, making it easy to determine which piece is being moved from square to square. It's this unique "addressing" that allows moves to be accurately recorded.

Captures are handled differently and the pawn gets the symbol P in English descriptive. Also, the symbol for check is *ch* rather than +.

Here is the same game you just looked at written in English descriptive notation:

1. P-K4 P-K4 2. N-KB3 P-Q3 3. P-Q4 B-N5 4. PxP BxN 5. QxB PxP 6. B-QB4 N-KB3 7. Q-QN3 Q-K2 8. N-B3 P-B3 9. B-KN5 P-N4 10. NxP PxN 11. BxPch QN-Q2 12. 0-0-0 R-Q1 13. RxN RxN 14. R-Q1 Q-K3 15. BxRch NxB 16. Q-N8ch NxQ 17. R-Q8 checkmate.

Other Notations

There are other notation systems you may come across from time to time. Spanish descriptive, Russian descriptive, or German descriptive are all very similar to English descriptive except that the piece symbols will correspond to the names of the pieces in those languages.

There is a special international correspondence notation system that is the simplest of all: Each square is assigned two numbers (both ranks and files are numbered) and moves are described as the square a piece or pawn has vacated and the square it moves to.

Forsyth Notation

There are notation systems for describing a chess position without bothering with the moves that led up to it. One such is Forsyth notation, in which each White piece or pawn is given as a capital letter and each Black piece or pawn as a lowercase letter. Empty squares are indicated by a number according to how many empty squares there are.

Chess notation, like music notation or mathematics notation, is quite specialized. It also has become standardized and even automatic with the rise of software, chess-playing computers, and the Internet. Thus you can read and write a universal language when you know chess notation.

Forsyth positions are set up like a diagram, with the White pieces at the bottom and the Black pieces at the top. Each row consists of a rank, starting with the eighth rank and continuing down to the first rank.

The final checkmate in the game we have been discussing looks like this in Forsyth notation:

1n1Rkb1r

p4ppp

4q3

4p1B1

4P3

8

PPP2PPP

2K5

Another Position Notation

Of course, it's just as easy to simply describe the pieces that are on the board and the squares they are on. Again, using the same checkmate position:

Black: Ke8, Qe6, Rh8, Bf8, Nb8, Pa7, e5, f7, g7, h7

White: Kc1, Rd8, Bg5, Pa2, b2, c2, e4, f2, g2, h2

FACT

There is one other type of chess notation: Braille. Yes, blind people can and do play chess. They don't play "blindfold," however, like a master at an exhibition. Instead, they use special boards and pieces that they are allowed to touch at all times, since their fingers are their eyes. They record and read chess games in Braille notation.

Diagrams

These notation systems for positions are all right as far as they go. But they won't be much help unless you have a chessboard and set to display the position. That is, unless you can easily visualize the position from the description. Not many people can do that readily.

So printed diagrams have come into use. These diagrams are simply a small picture of a chessboard with the pieces and pawns shown on their correct squares. You have already been making use of diagrams throughout this book, and will continue doing so.

Making diagrams was simply a matter of squishing a three-dimensional board with pieces and pawns into two dimensions. It was accomplished by picturing the board flat as seen from above and picturing the pieces as two-dimensional symbols of the actual pieces.

Representing a Game

Diagrams can be used in place of chess notation. The only problem is that they take up a lot of room, so printing costs and book or magazine weight and size are prohibitive. Here is the game we have been looking at so far in various notations, with a representation of each move shown with a new diagram:

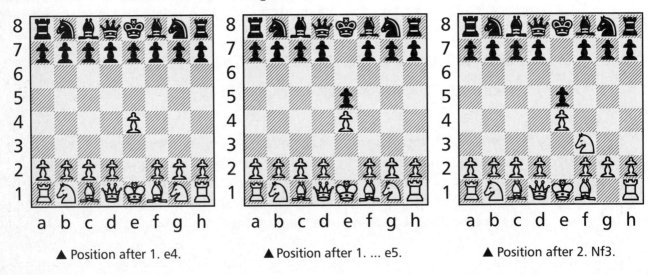

▲ Position after 1. e4. ▲ Position after 1. ... e5. ▲ Position after 2. Nf3.

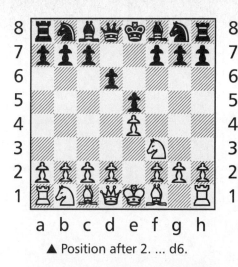

▲ Position after 2. ... d6.

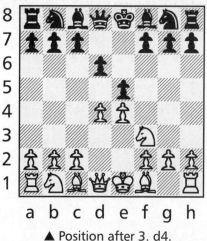

▲ Position after 3. d4.

▲ Position after 3. ... Bg4.

▲ Position after 4. dxe5.

▲ Position after 4. ... Bxf3.

▲ Position after 5. Qxf3.

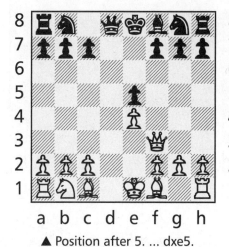

▲ Position after 5. ... dxe5.

▲ Position after 6. Bc4.

▲ Position after 6. ... Nf6.

▲ Position after 7. Qb3.

▲ Position after 7. ... Qe7.

▲ Position after 8. Nc3.

▲ Position after 8. ... c6.

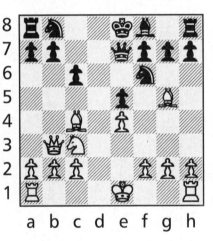

▲ Position after 9. Bg5.

▲ Position after 9. ... b5.

▲ Position after 10. Nxb5.

▲ Position after 10. ... cxb5.

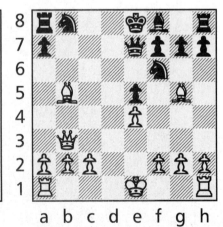

▲ Position after 11. Bxb5+.

▲ Position after 11. ... Nbd7.

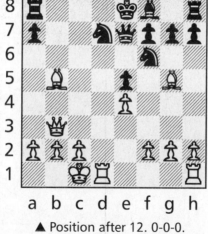

▲ Position after 12. 0-0-0.

▲ Position after 12. ... Rd8.

▲ Position after 13. Rxd7.

▲ Position after 13. ... Rxd7.

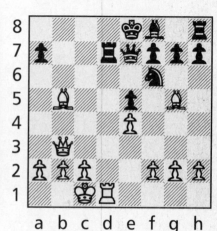

▲ Position after 14. Rd1.

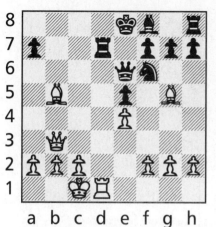

▲ Position after 14. ... Qe6.

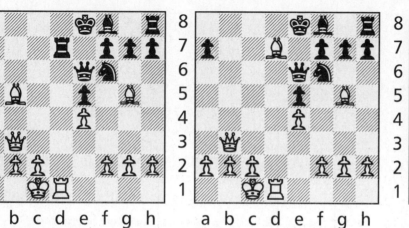

▲ Position after 15. Bxd7+.

▲ Position after 15. ... Nxd7.

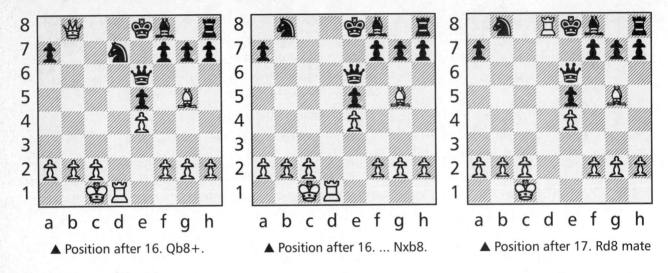

▲ Position after 16. Qb8+.   ▲ Position after 16. ... Nxb8.   ▲ Position after 17. Rd8 mate

Problems

Diagrams are also useful for positions for the student or interested reader to solve. These include positions from games where a combination will bring about a dramatic change in the position. They also include composed problems where the solver is asked to find a checkmate in a specified number of moves. Other composed problems will ask the solver to find a winning series of moves.

For the following diagrams, you are asked to find checkmate in one move. Answers are given after the problems.

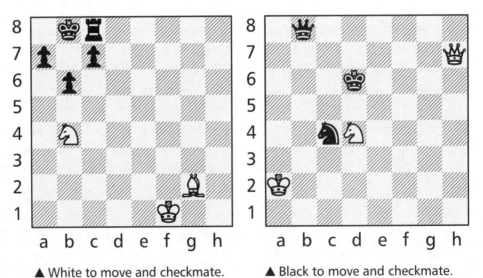

▲ White to move and checkmate.
Answer: 1.Na6 checkmate.

▲ Black to move and checkmate.
Answer: 1. ...Qb2 checkmate.

Game Scores

There are score sheets and score pads available at any tournament and for sale in stores and through the United States Chess Federation. You use these to write down a game in progress. The score will look somewhat different from those you see in magazines and books, but this is only because score sheets line up the moves in neat columns, rather than spread them out in a paragraph.

In a typical score sheet, there will be two sets of numbered double columns for a total number of four columns. The left-hand column is for White's moves. The column at the right of that one is for Black's moves. The third column is for later White moves. You will notice that they are numbered, continuing from the bottom of the first column. The last column is for later Black moves.

FACT

The game you have been looking at was played in 1858 at a Paris opera house during a performance of Rossini's *Il barbiere di Siviglia*. Paul Morphy, a young man from New Orleans and the strongest player in the world at the time, handled the White pieces. The Duke of Brunswick and Count Isouard consulted to come up with Black's replies.

The extra information asked for at the top is good to have in a tournament. Who played the White pieces? Who played the Black pieces? What were the ratings of the players? Where and when did the tournament take place? Pairing numbers and other information you may not understand are usually of interest only to the tournament director. There are lines below for the result of the game, which is a good bit of information for anybody intending to use the score of the game to know. Turn the page for a look at an official chess score sheet. Ⓔ

Official Score Sheet

White: _____

Black: _____

Section: _____ Board: _____ Round: _____ Date: _____

	White:	Black:		White:	Black:		White:	Black:
1.			23.			45.		
2.			24.			46.		
3.			25.			47.		
4.			26.			48.		
5.			27.			49.		
6.			28.			50.		
7.			29.			51.		
8.			30.			52.		
9.			31.			53.		
10.			32.			54.		
11.			33.			55.		
12.			34.			56.		
13.			35.			57.		
14.			36.			58.		
15.			37.			59.		
16.			38.			60.		
17.			39.			61.		
18.			40.			62.		
19.			41.			63.		
20.			42.			64.		
21.			43.			65.		
22.			44.			66.		

White wins   Black wins   Draw

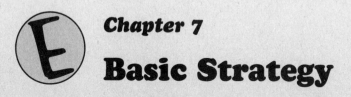

Chapter 7

Basic Strategy

Now that you know how to play chess and how to read and write chess, it is time to learn how to play chess with a reasonable degree of skill. This will also allow you to appreciate the skill and artistry of the masters. Anything beyond that is subject to talent and/or lots of structured work and play.

Principles to Follow

Before getting into the specifics of good play, we'll begin with a few general principles to follow during a game. These will help you in determining what move or plan to choose.

- The safety of both kings is the first priority.
- Greater force generally defeats lesser force.
- Control the center and you control the game.
- Control more squares and your opponent is smothered.
- Develop your pieces early and often.
- Long-range pieces need open lines to function well.
- Healthy pawns mean a healthy game.
- Whenever possible, operate with threats.

These are enough to start with. So let's look at them one at a time.

King Safety

The primacy of king safety is inherent in the rules. If your king is not safe, he may become trapped, and that means you lose. At the same time, you cannot win if your opponent's king remains safe. You must do something to trap the enemy monarch in order to win. So this principle is double-edged. It gives you a hint of what to keep in mind at all times during a chess game.

Your King

The first part of the principle implies safety for your own king. So the question becomes, "How do I make my king safe?" At the start of the game, he is surrounded by a queen, a bishop, and three pawns. Your king is in no immediate danger there.

The trouble starts with the other part of the principle. You begin the game by getting your pieces ready for an assault on the enemy king. But to do that, at least some of your pieces and pawns must necessarily leave the side of your own king. When that happens, he is no longer as safe as he was at the start of the game.

Castling

One of the best ways to ensure king safety is to tuck your big guy in a corner by way of castling. With three pawns in front of him and a rook by his side, and often a knight or even a bishop in the vicinity as well, your king has a good chance of maintaining reasonable safety for some time.

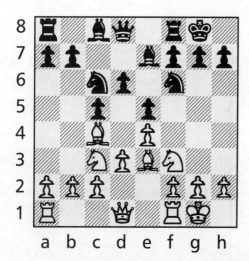

◄ Both kings are reasonably safe for the time being. It will be hard to storm such secure castles.

Later in the game, this fortress may be broken down and your king may have to leave. But as long as you make sure that doesn't occur until a number of pieces have been exchanged via capturing, you should be all right.

The king often comes out boldly later in the game. When the danger of checkmate is reduced because the enemy doesn't have many pieces (by then a number have been captured), you can use your king as an added attacking force. Just make sure the danger of checkmate is really significantly reduced!

The Other King

The other part of the first principle is the enemy king. You generally can't win the game if you can't checkmate him. But of course most opponents are going to be very annoying about not letting you near their royal leader.

Against a reasonably skilled opponent, you will not be able to put together a quick checkmating attack. So you have to build up your attack, using the other principles to gather your forces for the final blow.

Meanwhile, you have to keep in mind the final target as well as your own king's defense. It's a delicate balance, and you'll be confronted with it throughout any given game.

The Fastest Checkmate

Perhaps you are wondering what is the fastest checkmate. It is referred to as the Fool's Mate, and it takes a total of two moves! The fool plays White, and the game goes 1. f4 e6 2. g4 Qh4 checkmate.

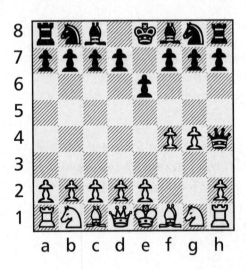

◀ White used his two moves to expose his king to the maximum, and Black checkmated him.

It takes a little longer for a fool to lose playing Black: 1. e4 e5 2. Qh5 Ke7 3. Qxe5 checkmate.

◀ Black's king blocks his own pieces from participating.

Another fast checkmate is called *Scholar's Mate*: 1. e4 e5 2. Bc4 Nc6 3. Qh5 Nf6 4. Qxf7 checkmate.

◀ The Black king cannot capture the White queen because that would expose him to check from the White bishop on c4.

Greater Force

Look at the checkmates on the previous pages and you can easily see what is meant by greater force. In all of them the poor king got clobbered by an enemy queen. In the first two, the fool opened up lines of attack for the enemy and closed off all retreat or blocking opportunities. In the third checkmate the triumphant queen swooped in with the help of a friendly bishop.

Piece Power

We know the queen is powerful, but just how powerful is she? And how strong are the other pieces and pawns in comparison? In order to compare them all, we need a measuring stick. So let's take the least powerful of all, the pawn, and use that as our measure. With that in mind, here are all the pieces listed in terms of their average power, expressed in terms of numbers of pawns:

- Knight = 3½
- Bishop = 3½
- Rook = 5

- Queen = 9
- King = infinity

There are several things about this list that may appear surprising or obscure. For instance, how can anything be worth half a pawn? And what is that about infinity?

A rook is generally stronger than a minor piece (a bishop or a knight). This difference is about 1½ pawns' worth, and is called the *Exchange*. This is not to be confused with the general term *exchange*, which refers to trading one piece for another. Thus you can exchange bishops, or exchange a queen for a rook and knight, but if you trade a rook for a knight you have given up the Exchange.

Unequal Balance

Sometimes this list is represented with the bishops and knights being worth only three pawns. This is not so far wrong, but we get messed up when we take three minor pieces and compare them to the queen. They are significantly stronger than her majesty. And a bishop and knight are generally a bit stronger than a rook and pawn. So the half-pawns are there to make it all come out a bit better.

It's hard to compare bishops and knights. Knights can cover the entire board eventually, while bishops can cover only half the squares. Yet bishops are long-range pieces and have a lot more immediate power than knights.

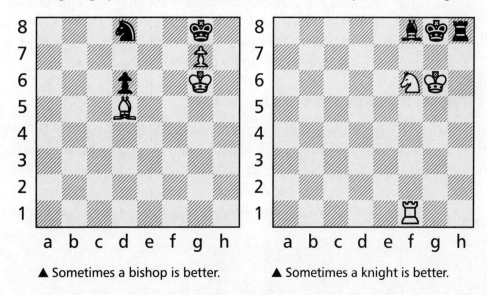

▲ Sometimes a bishop is better.   ▲ Sometimes a knight is better.

But when you fight with two bishops against two knights or a bishop and a knight, it is usually better to have the bishops. Together they have the long-range power *and* can cover every square on the board.

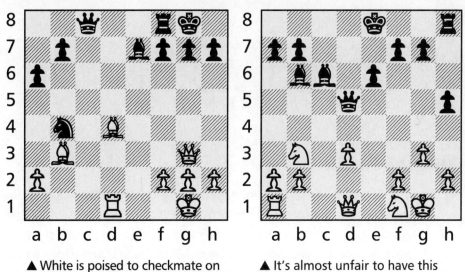

▲ White is poised to checkmate on g7. Note the power of both bishops.

▲ It's almost unfair to have this much power.

King Equal to Infinity

But what about the king being equal to infinity? That is in the very nature of chess. You can't put a value on the king, since he is not subject to capture. Thus all the pieces and pawns together won't equal his importance. As for his power when there are not many pieces left later in a game, it is something on the order of four pawns.

Greater Force Generally Wins

Greater force generally wins against lesser force. But only generally. In a sacrifice, a player gives up some greater force in order to bring about a concentration of force in a particular area of the board. For an example of a sacrifice, look at the game from Chapter 6. At the end of the game, Morphy gave up his queen for the chance to produce a checkmate.

◀ White plays 16. Qb8+!

Average Power

It is important to remember that these measurements are averages only. Rooks are generally much stronger than pawns, but what about a pawn about to promote to a queen? Bishops are about equal with knights, but what about a bishop locked behind its own pawns with nowhere to go compared with a knight that can hop over the whole board with impunity?

You can think of each piece and its average power as a potential. As long as you keep this in mind, you won't go too far wrong when exchanging a piece for a supposedly less powerful piece that is doing a lot of damage.

Chess has good bishops and bad bishops. A good bishop is one with open diagonals, many places to go, and pieces and pawns to annoy.

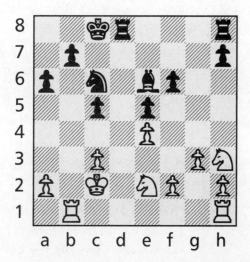

◀ The bishop gives White headaches on both sides of the board (a2 and h3).

A bad bishop is one that is trapped behind its own pawns. It doesn't have anything reasonable to do, and is sometimes referred to as a *tall pawn*, though sometimes even a pawn would be better. At least a pawn can move one square forward on a file.

◀ The bishop has nowhere to go, and blocks the b8-rook as well.

Control the Center

The importance of controlling the central squares is easy to illustrate. Just take an empty board and place a knight on the corner. Count up the number of squares it can jump to. The number is two.

Now place the knight somewhere along the middle of the edge of the board (first rank, eighth rank, a-file, h-file). You will find three or four possible squares for the knight now. That's twice the power.

Next, place the knight on one of the central squares. You will now see eight possible destinations for the knight. In other words, the knight has four times as much power in the center than it had on the edge of the board.

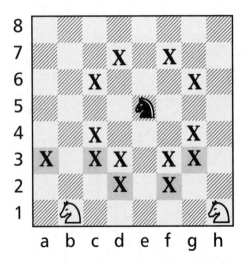

◀ The h1-knight has minimal power. The b1-knight is twice as many moves available. The e5-knight is twice as powerful as the b1-knight.

Try the bishop next. The results aren't as dramatic, but you will notice that the bishop gains in power from controlling seven squares to controlling thirteen squares.

ESSENTIAL

On an empty board, the rook seems to be just as powerful anywhere you place it. But that's not quite true. It can travel in four directions anywhere on the board except along the a-file, the h-file, the first rank, and the eighth rank—in other words, the edge of the board. So even the rook is stronger in the center.

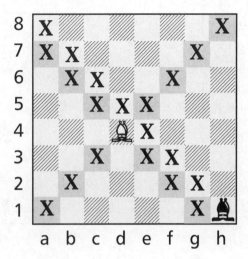

◀ Compare the power of the bishops and see why it's better to control central squares.

Busy Metropolis

The roads themselves are oriented toward the center, which we explored briefly in Chapter 2. Since there are more squares to visit from the center than from anywhere else, it shouldn't be too much of a surprise that the pieces are actually stronger in the center than they are anywhere else.

You can think of the chessboard as a hill, with the center being the highest elevation, and the outer squares the lowest elevation. That way chess becomes very like a case of king of the hill.

Counterattack in the Center

An attack on the flank, or side of the board, is best met by a counter-attack in the center. This is true even if the object of attack is your king. The point is that an attack against your king on the side of the board won't work unless your opponent can bring up reinforcements through the center.

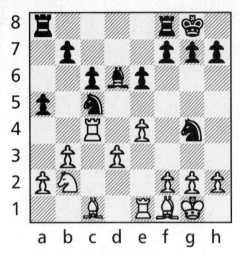

▲ White to move. Black threatens to capture the h-pawn with check.

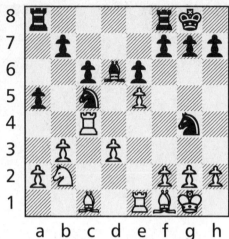

▲ White plays 1. e5!, giving both his rooks more squares and threatening to capture on d6 or g4.

Healthy Pieces

Think back to the table of piece power in terms of pawns. It should be clear by now why this table is only an average. Certainly a knight on e4 and a knight on a1 do not have the same power. As the game progresses, some pieces gain in power as they occupy the center or control it from afar while others suffer from a lack of good, healthy central air. There are other ways in which pieces gain and lose power during a game, but always keep in mind that they are generally strongest in or close to the center.

Even the lowly pawn benefits from being in the center. A pawn in the center can keep unwanted enemy pieces out. A pawn on the a-file or h-file just doesn't have the same power. There is only one direction to capture in instead of the normal two.

Control More Squares

This one is already familiar. Since there are sixty-four squares on the board, take control of thirty-three or more than half of them, and you will begin to smother your opponent. A smothered opponent is said to have a cramped game. There is a principle of strategy covering such a situation that is very useful to know. It comes in the following two parts.

When Cramped, Exchange Pieces

Since having a cramped position restricts your possible moves, your pieces do not operate at their most efficient level. A great way to fight out of such a situation is to exchange pieces.

You don't need anything fancy here. Just trade your minor pieces for your opponent's minor pieces and your rooks for your opponent's rooks. This gives your remaining pieces more room to breathe.

◀ Black to move relieves the cramp by exchanging: 1. ... Nxd4 2. Qxd4 Bxb5 3. Nxb5.

When Controlling Space, Avoid Exchanges

The other side of the principle is that when you control more squares than your opponent, avoid piece exchanges. This way your opponent will never get rid of all those cumbersome cramped pieces that step all over each other's toes.

Develop the Pieces

Playing a chess game is similar to coaching a sports team. You don't actually expose yourself to physical injury, but you do decide what your players will do. Your team in chess is not made of people, however. Rather, it is made of pieces and pawns.

Team Sport

So think of a team sport. Anything you prefer will do: football, soccer, hockey, or basketball. Any sport that pits a group of players against another group of players will be appropriate.

Let's take basketball for example. You are sending five players against the enemy five to score more points. So what do you think of this strategy: Send your best scorer out against the other team while the rest of your players watch the action?

It doesn't take a genius to figure out that such a strategy will not work very well. In fact, it's so bad, no coach will even think of trying it. Yet that is the very strategy many inexperienced chess players go for after learning of the tremendous power of the queen. Yes, she is strong, but she cannot do it all by herself.

A famous case of a player with a big lead in development (and, incidentally, controlling the center) carrying out a successful attack is Legal's Mate. This trap is named after De Kermur, Sire de Legal, a strong eighteenth-century player.

1. e4 e5 2. Nf3 d6 3. Bc4 a6 4. Nc3 Bg4.

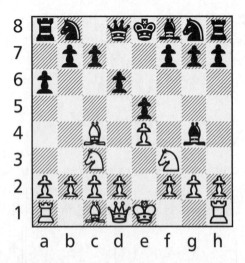

◄ Black has moved only pawns and now brings out a bishop where it is undefended. White has developed and played to control the center.

5. Nxe5! Bxd1 6. Bxf7+ Ke7 7. Nd5 checkmate.

◀ Three minor pieces and a pawn control the center and combine in checkmating the exposed Black king.

Build up Power

Since greater force generally defeats lesser force, and since you cannot gain greater force immediately against an experienced opponent, you will need to build up your force gradually. The way to do that is to develop a new piece with each move.

The trouble with the losing strategy in Legal's Mate is that Black only developed one piece during the entire game: The bishop moved to g4 and captured a queen. All the rest of Black's moves involved pushing pawns or getting the king out of check.

Meanwhile, White developed first a knight, then a bishop, then another knight, and finally began a powerful attack using those pieces and his control of the center. It's a clear case of what they call in basketball a three-on-one break.

Moving the Same Piece Again

A very good principle to keep in mind whenever you play a chess game is to move a different piece each time it is your move unless there is a particularly strong reason to move one you have already brought out. Then your problem becomes one of finding those strong reasons when you need to. These include:

- You will lose a piece or pawn if you don't move a developed piece.
- You can begin a winning attack by moving a developed piece.
- You can force your opponent to abandon his plan of attack by making a threat with a developed piece.
- There are no undeveloped pieces left to move.

A very good short-term goal to shoot for in the early part of the game is to connect your rooks. That means empty out the squares between your rooks on the first rank if you are White or on the eighth rank if you are Black. You can begin this by bringing out your minor pieces so that they control the central squares. Next, you can castle. That will connect your rooks and leave your king safe.

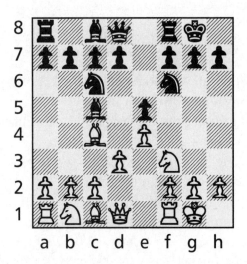

◀ Both sides have developed pieces and castled.

Developing pieces means not just getting them off their original position. It also means putting them where they will do some good. So you have to have a pretty good idea where that will be.

Long-Range Pieces Need Open Lines

Bishops, rooks, and queens won't ever do you any good unless they can oversee open lines. Any that sit behind friendly pawns represent unused potential. The thing to remember about them is that the bishops can come out into the melee early, while it is generally a good idea to hold back a bit on bringing out the rooks and queens.

The reason is simple. Bishops are less valuable than the major pieces, so can be exposed earlier. Also the rooks are a bit awkward with many pieces and pawns crowding the board. They are at their best later in the game when many pieces have been exchanged. The more ranks and files open up for them, the better off they are.

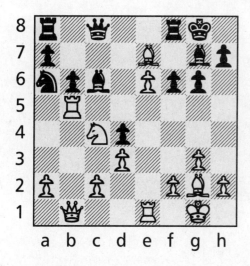

◄ White to move. Look at the White long-range pieces and note how many squares they control.

Fianchetto

Fianchetto is an Italian word meaning "flank development." It refers to the development of a bishop at g2, b2, b7, or g7. These squares are near the side of the board, but from them, the bishop commands one of the longest diagonals. Fianchettoed bishops control the center from the side of the board.

The problem with a fianchetto development is that an extra pawn move has to be made to make room for the bishop. This can cause problems, particularly if your king is nearby after castling.

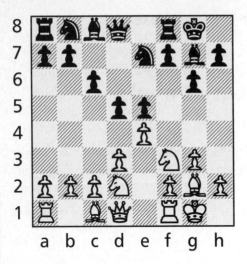

◀ Both sides have fianchettoed their bishops on the kingside.

Knights Need Outposts

An outpost is a square in or near the center that is protected by a friendly pawn. This is an ideal square for a short-hopping knight. Even better is a hole, which is an outpost in the opponent's territory that cannot be assailed by an enemy pawn.

◀ The knight on e5 is occupying an outpost. The knight on e4 is in a hole.

Keep in mind that minor pieces, and major pieces as well, need secure squares in order to function properly. If your opponent can drive your piece away from its open file, diagonal, or outpost with a pawn, or by attacking it with a piece where it cannot be defended, your piece is not secure.

Healthy and Unhealthy Pawns

So far the pieces have been the subject of discussion. But now we come to the pawns. As usual, they have to be handled differently in coming up with a viable strategy. The difference between pawns and pieces is that pawns have to be considered in groups. And each grouping has to be handled differently. Here are the main pawn groups:

- Pawn phalanx
- Pawn chain
- Doubled pawn
- Isolated pawn
- Passed pawn

Pawn Phalanx

A pawn phalanx is a group of two or more pawns on the same rank, on adjacent files. This formation is strong, particularly in the center or in your opponent's territory, because they control the row of squares directly in front of them. This keeps enemy pieces out.

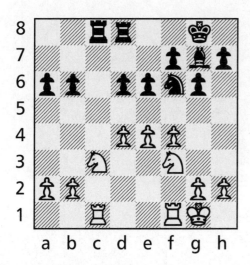

◄ White has a mighty pawn phalanx with his d-, e-, and f-pawns. Black has defensive pawn phalanxes on the a- and b-files and on the d- and e-files.

This formation can be vulnerable from the side or rear, as any pawns are. So if you control those squares, you have a powerful weapon. A great strategy when playing against a pawn phalanx is to force one of the pawns to move forward or capture something, thus breaking up the phalanx. A good way to break up an enemy pawn phalanx is to attack it with your own pawns.

ALERT!

If one of the pawns in a phalanx moves forward, we no longer have a phalanx. We then have a pawn chain.

Pawn Chain

One pawn defending another along a forward-looking diagonal is a pawn chain. There can be chains of four or five pawns lined up like this, each pawn behind defending the one in front.

The front pawn or pawns in a chain are strong. Capture one and you can expect a recapture from the pawn behind. But a pawn chain has a weakness. The base of the chain, or the pawn behind it all that supports the entire chain, can be vulnerable. So the best strategy when operating against a pawn chain is to attack the base of the chain. If the supporting pawn falls, the entire chain may crumble.

◀ Black's move should be 1. ... c5!, striking at d4, the base of White's pawn chain.

Doubled Pawn

A doubled pawn is a group of two friendly pawns on the same file. They can be strong along the adjacent files, since enemy pieces will find the squares there to be unsafe. But they are almost useless as attackers. The square directly in front of the doubled pawns is vulnerable, and they cannot form phalanxes unless allowed to capture something.

◄ White's c-pawns are doubled.

One byproduct of doubled pawns is the open file produced when making the capture that formed them in the first place. This is a great place for your rooks to get involved from.

Isolated Pawn

An isolated pawn is a group of one. An isolani (another way of referring to the isolated pawn) is a pawn with no friendly neighbors. Thus it can count on no pawn support. That makes it weak.

If the isolated pawn is in the center or deep in enemy territory, however, then it may be strong because of the disruptive influence it can have on the enemy. When a central isolated pawn springs up, it is often the focus of both player's plans.

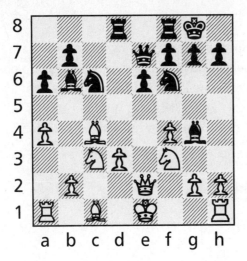

◀ White's d3-pawn is isolated.

The side with the isolani wants to push the pawn forward, further disrupting the enemy forces, while the side fighting against it wants to stop it from moving.

A great way to fight against a central isolated pawn is to blockade it. That means place a piece in front of it so it cannot move. The best piece for such a blockade is generally considered to be the knight.

◀ Black's d5-pawn is isolated. Note that White has blockaded it on d4 with a knight.

While the isolated pawn is thus blockaded, you can build up an attack against it, forcing the opponent to use pieces as defenders. Pieces that defend pawns aren't doing a lot of attacking.

Passed Pawn

A passed pawn is one that is free from any enemy pawn interference. As it marches up the board, the passed pawn will encounter no enemy pawns, either on its own file or on either adjacent file.

◀ White's d5-pawn is passed.

The tremendous strength of a passed pawn is that it is a candidate to promote. The further it has advanced up the board, the more menacing it becomes. Therefore, a passed pawn is said to have a lust to expand. Besides capturing such a pawn, the next best way of dealing with it is to blockade, just like with an isolated pawn.

A pawn majority is a case of two pawns against one pawn or three pawns against two pawns, etc., on one side of the board. The object of a pawn majority is to produce a strong passed pawn.

ALERT!

The strength of a passed pawn is not necessarily that it will march up the board and promote. Rather, it can often be strong because enemy pieces are tied up stopping it. Thus, those pieces are not available for other duties.

◀ White has a pawn majority on the queenside.

One way to break up such a majority is to attack the stronger party with the weaker party. This is the minority attack. The object of a minority attack is to produce a weak isolated pawn to play against.

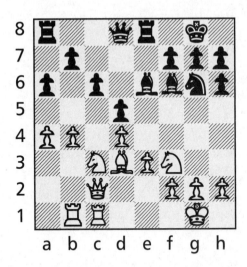

◀ White is poised for the minority attack with 1. b5!

Whenever Possible, Operate with Threats

This is so important that it gets its own chapter. There are many chess books written on this topic, and paying attention to threats may be the biggest difference between strong and weak players.

Very simply, if you don't notice that your queen is in danger when you make your move, you might lose her. If you don't notice that you can checkmate you opponent's king in two moves, you may not go on to win the game. If you don't notice that your king is about to come under attack, you may not be able to find a good defense.

If this sounds like you have to pay close attention to possible threats on every move of every game, that's because it is the only way to become a strong player. Sherlock Holmes, with his excellent eye for minute detail and his awareness of clues that everyone could see but few could interpret, would have made a strong chess player.

Chapter 8

Threats

Everything up to here has been nothing more than necessary preparation for good chess play. In order to take it up a notch and dramatically improve your technique, you need to know how to look ahead a few moves to predict what might happen.

Forcing Moves

Since there are on average about forty or more possible moves in most chess positions, looking ahead even one move becomes very difficult if done randomly. Trying to look two or three moves ahead in this fashion is virtually impossible: to each of my forty possible moves my opponent has forty possible replies. That comes out to 1,600 possible moves. And that is looking exactly one move ahead.

This is fine for a brute force computer, but impossible for a human brain. Fortunately, this sort of number crunching is not necessary or even desirable in the pursuit of good chess play.

In order to drastically cut down on the number of moves we need to look at in predicting the near future of a game, we need to find a device that limits our opponent's possible replies. That device is the use of forcing moves.

A forcing move is a move that forces our opponent to respond. An example of a forcing move that you already know about is check. When the enemy is in check, his possible replies are limited to the available ways to get out of check.

Manageable Look-Ahead

By using forcing moves you put your opponent in a quandary. He no longer has the usual forty or so moves to choose from. He must restrict himself to the available moves that get him out of whatever fix you have put him in. That may be as little as two or three moves he will have to choose between. That will certainly make preparing your reply to either of two or three moves by your opponent more possible! Keeping five to ten possible moves in mind may not be easy, but it sure is a lot more possible than trying to keep up with 500 to 1,000 possible moves!

If your opponent isn't very experienced, he might not know that your move was forcing. In that case, you won't do so well in predicting his moves, but that will present no special problem because you were counting on good moves from your opponent. If a poor move comes in its place, all the better.

Other Threats

A check is a direct threat to the king. Any move that threatens to capture a piece or a pawn next turn can have a similar effect. If your opponent does not want to lose that piece or pawn, she will have to meet the threat in some way.

◀ White threatens to capture the undefended bishop on b4.

A threat to promote a pawn is also a great way to cut down on your opponent's possible replies. Since a pawn promotion generally means trading a pawn for a queen, this can usually not be ignored.

There are still other threats that, while not so dramatic as threats to capture or promote, can still be used to cut down on your opponent's possibilities. These include threats to double or isolate the enemy pawns or a threat to get a knight to a fine outpost square. You can threaten to control the center or to bring more pieces in play than your opponent has available.

Recognizing threats is essential to good chess play. Whether it is a queen or a key square under fire or the possibility of getting one of your pieces tied up in defense, you can't do anything about a threat if you don't know it is there.

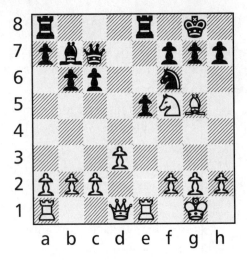

◀ White threatens to destroy the Black king's protection by 1. Bxf6.

Anything that helps your position or hurts your opponent's position or both is generally worth threatening.

How to Meet a Threat

A threat to capture something can be viewed as something like a minor check. As such there are five possible ways to meet a threat to capture something other than a king. The first three are already familiar:

1. Capture the threatening piece or pawn.

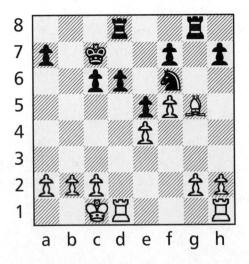

◀ The threat is 2. Bxf6. Take care of it by playing 1. ... Rxg5.

2. Block the path of the long-range attacker.

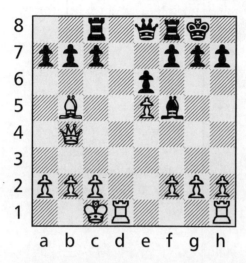

◀ Black's queen is threatened. Block the path of the b5-bishop with 1. ... c6.

3. Move the threatened piece or pawn.

◀ Black's knight is threatened. Move it to a safe square, such as 1. ... Nd7.

ALERT!

When moving a threatened piece or pawn, take particular care that the new square is indeed a safe one. It won't help to go from the frying pan into the fire.

These are the very same devices we use to get out of check. But when the object of the threat is not a king, two other ways to deal with it pop up:

4. Defend the threatened piece or pawn.

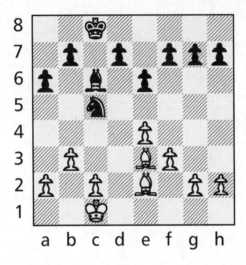

◀ Defend the threatened knight with 1. ... d6. If White captures with 2. Bxc5, Black simply recaptures with 2. ... dxc5.

5. Ignore the threat.

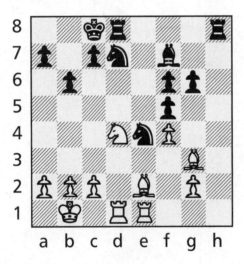

◀ The g3-bishop is under attack, but White ignores it and attacks with 1. Ba6+ Kb8 2. Nc6+ Ka8 3. Nxd8. Black's f7-bishop and d7-knight are now under attack.

Defend

This is something you can't even think of doing when your king is under attack. But anything else can be defended by setting up a possible recapture. All right, so your knight is captured. As long as you get equivalent value, no harm is done. If the attacking piece is a bishop, you will wind up with a fair exchange after the captures are made.

The same goes if your queen is the piece under attack. As long as you can get your opponent's queen or some equivalent value (two rooks, two minor pieces and two pawns, etc.) you will have defended the threat successfully.

◀ Black gets two rooks for his queen by exchanging with 1. ... Qxe1t 2. Nxe1 Rxd2.

Make sure you get equivalent value when defending against a threat to capture. If a bishop is attacking your rook, defending the rook will not do. You lose your rook and gain a bishop. You have lost the Exchange.

◀ Black loses the Exchange by defending with 1. ... Nc7 2. Bxe6 Nxe6. It's better to move the rook with 1. ... Rd6 2. Rxd6 Nxd6, with an even trade.

Ignore

This is another device you cannot use when the threat is to your king. But anything else is fair. Of course, if your queen is being threatened with capture and you just go about your business as if nothing has happened, you will lose your queen. This is true whether or not you saw the capture coming. There's not a whole lot of profit there.

What ignoring the threat can accomplish, however, is explained best by the old adage, "The best defense is a good attack." Thus you can successfully ignore an attack to your queen by putting your opponent's king in check. Or you can ignore an attack to your rook by attacking your opponent's queen. Or by preparing to promote a pawn.

You get the idea. By threatening something more valuable, you can avoid bothering with the defense. Just make sure your attack really is worth more, in case your opponent ignores your attack in turn.

◀ White ignores the threat to his g5-knight and plays 1. Qf3, threatening Black's queen. After 1. ... Qxf3, he recaptures and saves the knight by playing 2. Nxf3.

Just remember that after the Zwischenzug the original threat may still be there. If it is, you will have to come up with another way to deal with it. Even, perhaps, another Zwischenzug.

Ignoring a threat temporarily in order to threaten something else of more value is known as a *Zwischenzug*. That's a German word for "in-between move."

◀ White ignores the threat to his queen and plays 1. exf6 Nxd4 2. fxe7, which gets the queen back.

En Prise

En prise is another French phrase. It means "in take" and refers to a situation where there is a piece or pawn threatened with capture at a time when there is no defender ready to recapture. Such a piece or pawn is also said to be hanging or dangling.

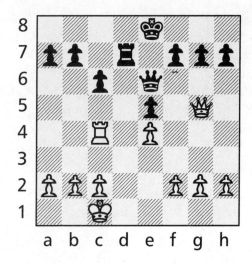

◀ White's rook is en prise.

The best advice for dealing with en prise pieces or pawns is to pay attention to them. If you don't notice a hanging piece you probably won't do anything about it. Yet there are usually several good ways to address the problem.

One very good way to keep out of en prise trouble is to make sure all your pieces and pawns are defended at all times. That may not always be possible, but by striving for such a situation you can drastically cut down on accidentally losing such a dangler.

A word of caution: If you are playing an experienced opponent and she leaves a piece en prise, don't immediately snatch it up. There may be a purpose behind this seeming carelessness. Chess is filled with traps in which an innocent-looking capture actually loses the game through a counterattack. It's up to you to find such traps in your games.

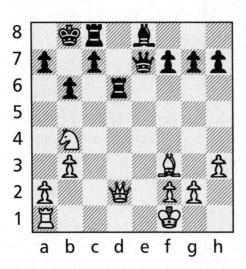

◄ Should Black capture the en prise queen? No! After 1. ... Rxd2, White plays 2. Na6 checkmate.

Another thing to be aware of is that the en prise disease can affect your opponent as well as you. Always be aware of any unprotected piece or pawn, regardless of its color.

Convergence

This one amounts to the same thing as en prise, but it's trickier to recognize. Convergence refers to a situation where there are two pieces (or pawns) threatening to capture a piece or pawn that has only one defender. By extension, there can be more than two attackers and more than one defender, but there are always more attackers than defenders in convergence.

◀ The bishop and queen converge on f7, which is only defended by the king.

It's Defended

The very fact that the object of the converging attack is defended is what throws off the inexperienced player. Yes, it is defended, but the defense is insufficient.

ESSENTIAL

Being able to look at positions that have not happened yet and compare them to the position that is actually in front of you is an essential skill in chess. A good drill is to set up any position that contains a convergence and try to figure out all the captures in your head. Then play them out, and see how close you came to the positions that actually emerge.

In order to appreciate the power of convergence, you will have to learn to look ahead at least two moves. If the convergence contains three attackers and two defenders, you will need to look ahead at least three moves. But since those moves are all captures, and the captures all take place on the same square, you should be able to manage it.

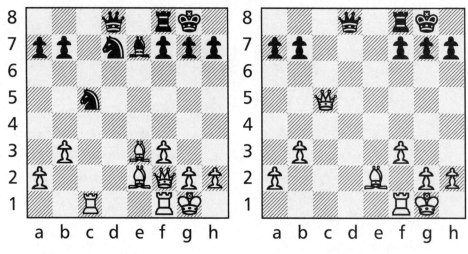

▲ White has three attackers on the c5-knight, while Black has only two defenders. The play goes 1. Bxc5 Nxc5 2. Rxc5 Bxc5 3. Qxc5.

▲ White winds up a piece ahead.

Unit Value

Another tricky part of convergence is when the attacking units, or even just one of the attacking units, are more valuable than the defending units. In those cases, a simple count of attackers and defenders is not sufficient.

Again, you need to be able to look ahead the two or three moves that include all the captures. But you also need to be able to judge who has gotten the better of the deal *after* the entire series of exchanges. For that, you need to go back to simple counting.

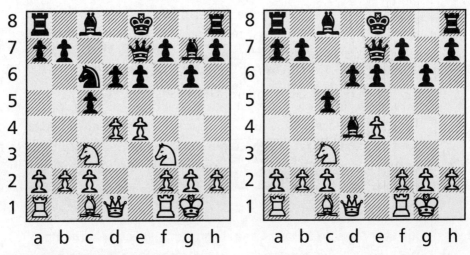

▲ Black threatens to capture three times on d4, but White has only two defenders. The play goes 1. ... Nxd4 2. Nxd4 Bxd4.

▲ Now everybody can see that the queen shouldn't capture on d4.

Blindfold Play

This is a good place to bring up an excellent training tool. Your thoughts during a chess game will be filled with looking at possible sequences of moves in your head while an actual position is before you. Getting better at chess is at least partially based on your ability to see these sequences farther into the game. Improvement is also dependent upon seeing these sequences more clearly in your head.

Therefore, an attempt to stretch out that ability should be an excellent exercise. So what could be better than an attempt to play an entire game without looking at a board or pieces?

Too Difficult!

If you think this exercise is a bit too difficult for one who has just begun trying to understand what chess is all about, you're right. Don't expect to complete a whole game on your first try. And don't expect to play very well either. Neither completing the game nor playing well are the goal at this point.

The Goal

Trying to get as far as you can while playing as well as you can is what stretches your imaginative capacity. After working on it, perhaps with numerous tries, you may eventually complete an entire game or play a reasonably error-free series of moves. But that really doesn't matter.

What matters is that you will improve your look-ahead ability with this exercise, and you will begin to see series of moves in your games a bit deeper and with more clarity. And that is the real goal of this blindfold exercise.

FACT

Every year in Monte Carlo, Monaco, a special tournament takes place among many of the world's leading grandmasters. Melody-Amber is a series of two tournaments, in which the grandmasters compete with each other in rapid chess and in blindfold rapid. That last is what makes this event unique. The players get to see a chessboard, but they have no pieces, and must key in their moves via computer.

Battery

This is a special type of convergence. In a battery, two friendly pieces line up to attack a piece or pawn that doesn't have enough defenders. The attacker in front can be a rook, bishop, queen, or pawn. Anything that moves in straight lines (ranks, files, or diagonals) will do, except for the king.

ALERT!

A famous example of a battery is the doubled rooks on an open file. It's also very good to have two rooks on the same rank, especially on one of your opponent's home ranks. That way, one rook can back up the other. A particularly strong form of this is the tripled major pieces, either on a rank or a file, with the queen backing up the rooks.

The Front Unit

Knight's don't ever operate as part of a battery because they don't use the normal straight-line highways. Kings can't be part of a battery for another reason. They move in straight lines all right, but the front unit in a battery must be expendable.

The way a battery operates is that the front unit directly threatens to capture something. After the expected recapture (this explains why a king can't be the guy for such a job) the back piece comes into play, following up with another capture.

In a normal convergence, the two attackers look in from different directions. In a battery, the direction and indeed the very highway is the same for both attackers.

The Back Piece

By the very nature of a battery, the rear unit must be a long-range piece. Therefore, bishops, rooks, and queens are often placed behind other friendly pieces and pawns in order to back them up.

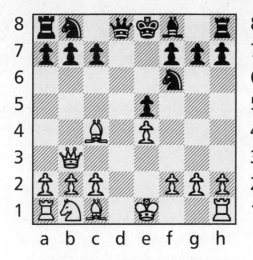

▲ The queen on b3 backs up the c4-bishop for a battery aimed at f7.

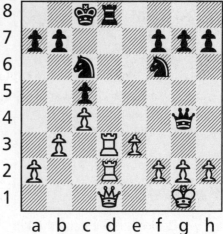

▲ White has a triple battery on the d-file, aiming at the d8-rook. Black has only two defenders for d8.

The most virulent form of doubled rooks is the "blind pigs on the seventh." That refers to two White rooks lined up on the seventh rank, where all the opponent pawns lack any pawn support. Of course, two Black rooks on the second rank have the same effect.

Another formidable battery is the queen-bishop duo. With the bishop in front many things can be threatened. With the queen in front, there are many cases of checkmate threats lurking. It's a good one to know.

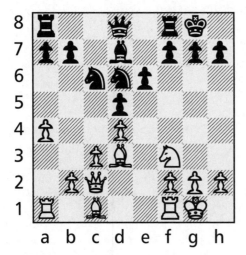

▲ White threatens to capture on h7 with check due to his queen-bishop battery.

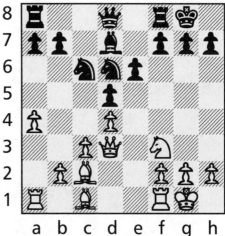

▲ White threatens checkmate on h7 due to his queen-bishop battery with the queen in front.

Promotion

Besides threatening the king, checkmate, stalemate, and capturing pieces or pawns, a very dangerous threat is that of pawn promotion. This one is perhaps a little more sophisticated than you might think. The threat of promotion does not only refer to a pawn on the seventh or second rank poised for the coming coronation. It also refers to any passed pawn that is not properly restrained.

Pawn Majority

We have already met the pawn majority in the last chapter. So we know that a pawn majority is more pawns of one color than of the other color on one side of the board. The strength of such a majority is that after the pawns are traded off, one for another, a lone pawn will emerge. That will be a passed pawn, which means it is a pawn that will eventually threaten to promote.

Pawn majorities, and especially passed pawns, are particularly strong in the endgame, when most of the pieces have been exchanged off and are gone. In such cases, the kings become strong pieces, and can help a pawn to promote or help stop a pawn from promoting.

Candidate

The way to use a pawn majority is to move up the candidate passed pawn first. The candidate is the one with no enemy pawns on the same file.

◄ The entire pawn majority continues to advance up the board, with the candidate leading the way. The b-pawn is the candidate. 1. b5 Kg6 2. a5 Kf6 3. b6 axb6 4. axb6 Ke6 5. b7 Kd6 6. b8=Q.

Outside Passed Pawn

This is a special case that often comes out of an outside pawn majority. The "outside" refers to the side of the board away from the kings. So if the kings are busy on the kingside, a pawn majority on the queenside will produce an outside or distant passed pawn. The way to use such a pawn is to march it forward, forcing the enemy king to come over to stop it. Then your own king can mop up the pawns the enemy king was forced to abandon.

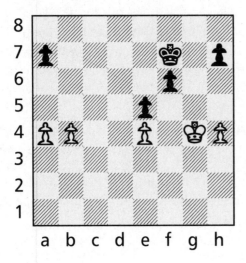

◄ 1. b5 Ke6 2. a5 Kd6 3. b6 axb6 4. axb6 Kc6 5. b7 Kxb7 6. Kf5 and the White king dines on Black's pawns.

Combinations

Here are some combinations in which a passed pawn is created and/or promotes.

ALERT!

Keep in mind the pawn's ability to underpromote. Probably 99 percent of the time an underpromotion will not be a real threat. But every once in a while a knight or a rook could destroy your position, while a queen won't make much difference. Take each position on its own merit.

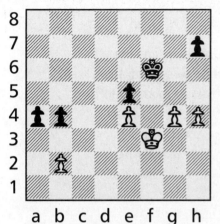

▲ Black to move plays 1. ...
a3 and keeps marching the
pawn to a1.

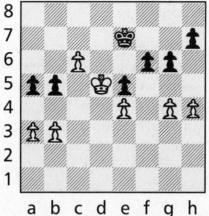

▲ White plays 1. Kc5 and
mops up the queenside
pawns. There is no need to
push his passed pawn: The
Black king will have to keep a
sharp eye on it, so it won't
be able to do any damage.

▲ White breaks through with
1. b6! axb6 2. c6! bxc6 3. a6
and the a-pawn marches
through. Or 1. b6! cxb6 2.
a6! bxa6 3. c6 and the c-
pawn marches through.

Even though there are a few pieces left, the threat of promoting a
pawn makes the following combination possible.

◀ Black to move wins with 1. ...
h3! And there is no way to stop
one of the Black pawns from
safely promoting.

Opposition

When only kings and pawns are left, a peculiarity of the kings often comes into play. This is called the *opposition*, and occurs when the kings get as close to each other as they can come. That means there is one rank, file, or diagonal between them.

The nature of chess is such that the kings can't approach any closer, since that would mean moving into check. This makes the squares between the kings at closest approach an impenetrable barrier. And that being the case, it is a barrier you can use.

Who Is on Move?

When kings face off, the one who is on move will have to give way. Therefore, you want to set up an opposition only when it is your opponent's turn to move.

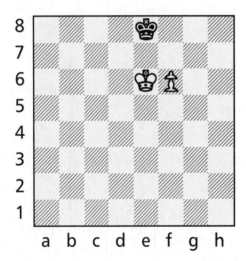

◄ White to move results in a draw by stalemate: 1. f7t Kf8 2. Kf6 stalemate. Black to move results in a White win by 1. ... Kf8 2. f7 Kg7 3. Ke7 and the pawn safely promotes.

Opposition can help you checkmate the enemy king or it can help you promote a pawn. We'll leave the checkmate for the next chapter. Right now, let's see how using the opposition can help you promote a pawn.

When your king is too far away from the passed pawn to be of any service, you may still get to safely promote it. Just make sure the enemy king is outside the square of the pawn. That means you count the number of squares forward it takes to promote the pawn and draw an imaginary line of the same length along the rank or diagonal leading to your opponent's king. If that king is outside the line, your pawn will promote safely.

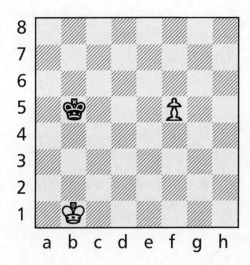

◄ White to move wins with 1. f6 and the pawn cannot be caught. Black to move draws by stepping into the square of the pawn with 1. ... Kc5.

Keep Your King in Front of the Pawn

This is the key to promoting a pawn in king-and-pawn endings. The pawn needs to move forward in order to promote, so those forward squares are the ones needing support.

If you can control the promotion square, your pawn will promote safely. If you cannot, your pawn will not get through.

It may seem anti-intuitive to move the king in front of the pawn that you want to push forward. But the squares the pawn has to cover on the way to promotion must belong to you, or the little guy will never make it. Control those squares and you control the game.

Here is an example of winning with the use of opposition when you have a king and pawn versus a lone king.

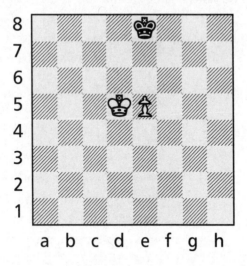

◀ White to move wins with 1. Ke6 Kd8 2. Kf7 and the pawn marches through.

This is an example of stopping an enemy pawn from promoting with your lone king using opposition.

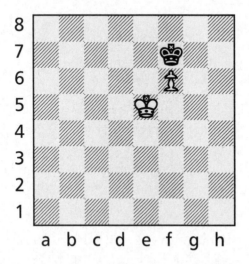

◀ Black to move draws with 1. ... Kf8! 2. Ke6 Ke8 3. f7+ Kf8 4. Kf6 stalemate.

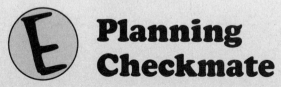

Chapter 9

Planning Checkmate

Checkmates don't just happen randomly. You have to set them up by visualizing them in advance. Then you have to find a way to get your opponent to cooperate. This isn't easy, since nobody wants to get checkmated. In other words, you have to plan for checkmates.

The Basic Checkmates

The first thing you need to plan checkmate is to know just what a checkmate looks like. Therefore, here are a number of checkmates using the various pieces and pawns. All nonessential pieces and pawns are removed so you just see the pure checkmate. Even the White king is missing in most cases.

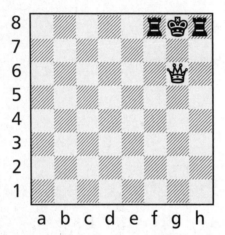

◀ The queen covers the g-file as well as the seventh rank escape squares. Black's rooks cover the other escape squares.

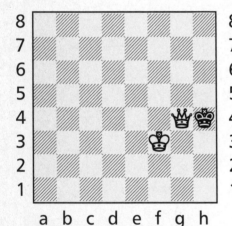

▲ The queen covers everywhere the Black king could go, except her own square, g4. That is covered by the White king.

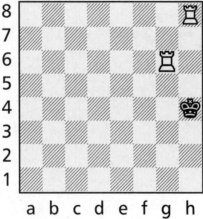

▲ The h8-rook covers all h-file squares, while the g6-rook covers all g-file escape squares.

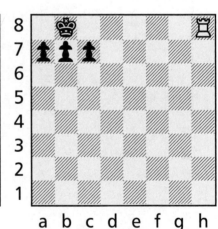

▲ The rook covers all eighth-rank squares, while the seventh rank is denied to the king by his own pawns.

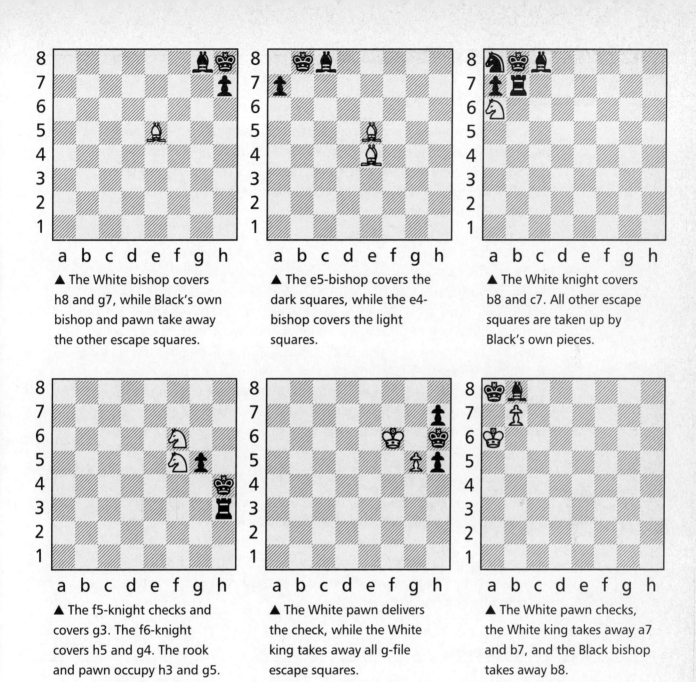

▲ The White bishop covers h8 and g7, while Black's own bishop and pawn take away the other escape squares.

▲ The e5-bishop covers the dark squares, while the e4-bishop covers the light squares.

▲ The White knight covers b8 and c7. All other escape squares are taken up by Black's own pieces.

▲ The f5-knight checks and covers g3. The f6-knight covers h5 and g4. The rook and pawn occupy h3 and g5.

▲ The White pawn delivers the check, while the White king takes away all g-file escape squares.

▲ The White pawn checks, the White king takes away a7 and b7, and the Black bishop takes away b8.

To understand how to bring about these checkmates, you need to be able to visualize the final checkmate. When you can do that, you will be able to find a lurking checkmate anytime there is a chance for one. Simply look for all the possible checks and determine if there is a way out. If not, you have found a checkmate!

Definition

Basic checkmates are those produced with the minimum amount of material: the king getting checkmated and the king and piece or pieces needed to produce the checkmates are the only pieces occupying the board. There are no pawns on the board in these basic checkmate positions. These include:

- Two rooks
- Rook and king
- Queen and king

- Two bishops and king
- Bishop, knight, and king

Only in the first of the list, the one involving two rooks, is the strong side's king unnecessary. There is also queen and rook or two queens, but these are redundant. You will notice that two knights and king do not appear on the list. You can checkmate an inattentive opponent using only those pieces, but an experienced player will always be able to slip away. There is no way to force checkmate with only two knights and king against a lone king.

Checkmates don't spring up on inspiration when you want them to. You have to plan for them well in advance. The first step is to know what the checkmates look like. The next step is to find checkmates lurking on the very next move. The third and hardest phase is to recognize a checkmate pattern forming in the future and play to bring it about.

Some Examples

Here are some positions where a checkmate waits to be found on the next move. All you have to do is find the right check. It is White to move and checkmate Black in each case.

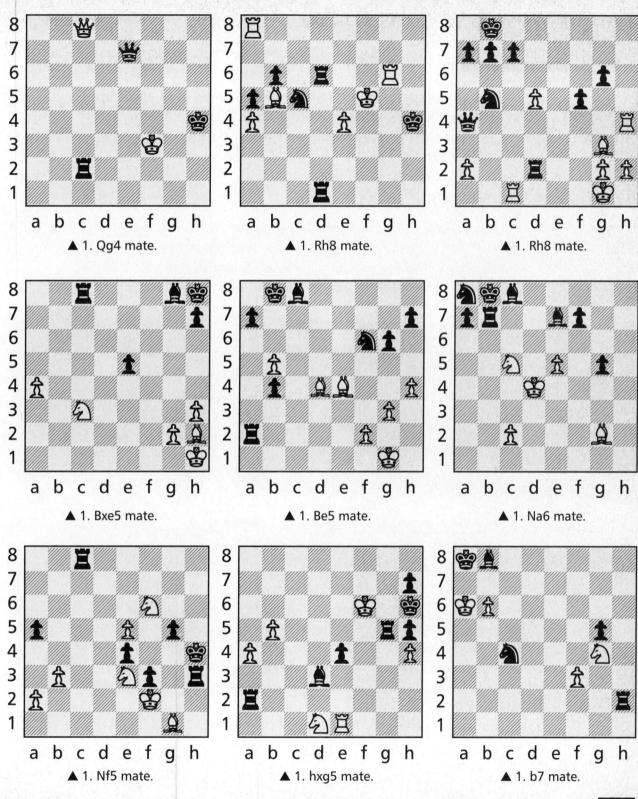

▲ 1. Qg4 mate.

▲ 1. Rh8 mate.

▲ 1. Rh8 mate.

▲ 1. Bxe5 mate.

▲ 1. Be5 mate.

▲ 1. Na6 mate.

▲ 1. Nf5 mate.

▲ 1. hxg5 mate.

▲ 1. b7 mate.

Two Rooks

This is the simplest and the easiest to execute of the basic checkmates. It is the same whether we use two rooks, two queens, or rook and queen. The strong king isn't even necessary, and could get in the way if you aren't careful.

The Checkmate

The final checkmate will have the weak king on the edge of the board. Either the a-file or the h-file or the first rank or the eighth rank will do. But don't think you can checkmate a king in the middle of the board unless he cooperates or you use your own king to help.

◄ The checkmated king is on the edge of the board. Note that the rooks take away the seventh and eighth ranks.

The reason you need to herd the weak king to the side of the board or, even better, a corner of the board, is that he has too many escape squares when he is in the center. The weak king is hard to trap in the center just because he has so many possibilities. Naturally, any intelligent weak king is going to try to stay in or near the center in order to preserve his life, so your plan must be to induce him to the side or corner and checkmate him there.

The Plan

The lumbering giants can herd the king to the side of the board by what is sometimes referred to as *bicycle pedaling*. One full rank (or file) is first taken away from the weak king by one of the rooks. Then the next rank is taken away by the other rook, then the next by the first rook, until the poor beleaguered fellow comes to the edge of the board. At that time he has no further recourse and is checkmated.

Here's how it works:

◀ The game continues 1. Ra4 Kg5 2. Rb5+ Kf6 3. Ra6+ Ke7 4. Rb7+ Kd8 5. Ra8 checkmate.

FACT

Distance is a useful protection for rooks, especially when fighting against any piece that can move along diagonals, such as a king.

Rook and King

This is trickier and takes a little longer, but the checkmate is always there if you know what you are doing. The checkmate will look something like this:

▲ Once again, the checkmated king is on the edge of the board. The rook takes away the h-file, while the White king takes away the g-file.

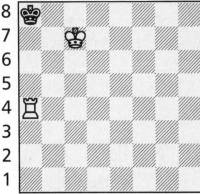

▲ The rook takes away the a-file, while the White king covers the b-file.

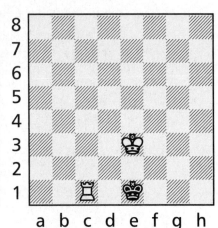

▲ The rook covers the first rank while the White king takes away second-rank squares.

Opposition

You've already encountered opposition in the last chapter. There you used it to help shepherd a pawn to the promotion square or to prevent a pawn from getting to the promotion square.

FACT

There are many books devoted to checkmate on the market. The simplest are those of A. J. Gillam, who fills up his books with checkmate positions or positions one move from checkmate. Others include *Bobby Fischer Teaches Chess*, which is a step-by-step explanation of how to find the lurking checkmating patterns in positions two and three moves away from the final checkmate.

The way to use it in king and rook versus rook positions is to take an entire rank or file away from the opposing king using the opposition. Thus, your king fulfills the role of one of the rooks in the two-rook checkmate.

The idea of gradually taking squares away from the weak king is the whole key to this checkmate plan. The weapons you use are the opposition and the tremendous long-range power of the rook, which can take away an entire file or rank from the lone weak king, or lose a move in order to persuade that monarch to step into the opposition himself. When your prey is finally in jail, with nowhere left to go, it is time for the checkmate.

Taking Squares Away

Here's how to do it. This is really nothing more than a slower way to execute the two-rook checkmate. It's just that your king isn't as powerful as the other rook was. So you have to use the opposition to take a rank or file away from the weak king.

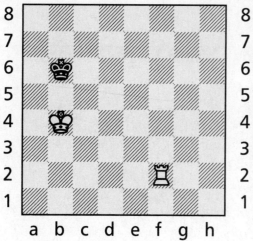

▲ Kings already in opposition.
1. Rf6+ Kc7 2. Kc5 Kd7.

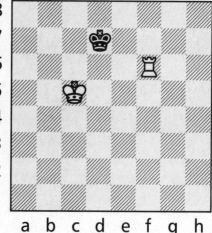

▲ Kings not yet in opposition.
3. Kd5 Ke7 4. Rf1.

This last move is the key. White does not move into the opposition. Rather, he gently persuades Black to move into the opposition himself by dropping back with his rook.

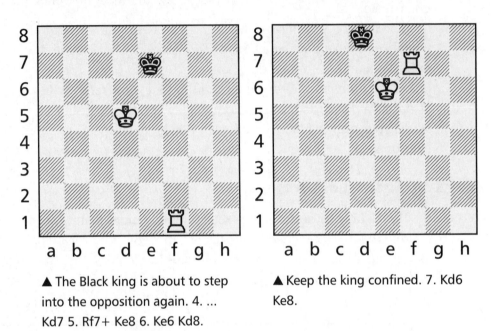

▲ The Black king is about to step into the opposition again. 4. ... Kd7 5. Rf7+ Ke8 6. Ke6 Kd8.

▲ Keep the king confined. 7. Kd6 Ke8.

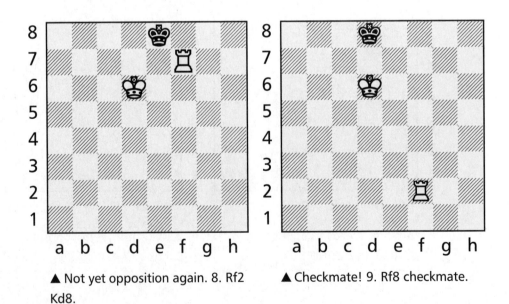

▲ Not yet opposition again. 8. Rf2 Kd8.

▲ Checkmate! 9. Rf8 checkmate.

The Back Rank Mate

The back rank mate, also referred to as the *corridor mate*, is one that can be executed only by a major piece. It is the mate that ends the king and major piece against king positions. It can take place on a side file as well as a side rank. But it can also come about when the next file or rank is denied the checkmated king by something other than an enemy king and opposition. Following are some examples.

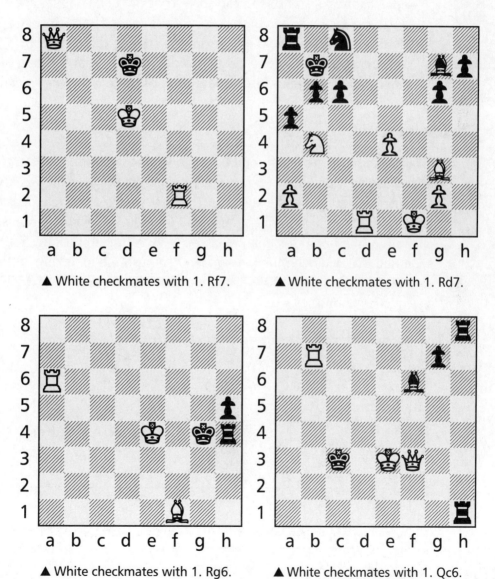

▲ White checkmates with 1. Rf7.

▲ White checkmates with 1. Rd7.

▲ White checkmates with 1. Rg6.

▲ White checkmates with 1. Qc6.

Queen and King

Since a queen is more powerful than a rook, you would think that checkmating with king and queen would be easier than checkmating with king and rook. Well, yes, that's true, and you can generally checkmate the lone king much faster with king and queen. But it's also trickier.

Since a lone rook and king can force checkmate against a lone king, and a lone queen and king can force checkmate against a lone king, it follows that a lone pawn and king can also force checkmate against a lone king. Provided, that is, that the king and pawn can combine to force a safe promotion to a rook or queen.

Stalemate!

The reason it is trickier to checkmate with a queen than with a rook is because the tremendous power of the queen often gives the weak king a chance to set up a stalemate trap. The best way to show that possibility is to try to checkmate a lone king with a lone queen. Nothing else is allowed on the board for this exercise—not even the strong king. You will soon find that, although the lone queen can push the lone king to the side of the board, there is never a checkmate. There are, however, stalemate opportunities.

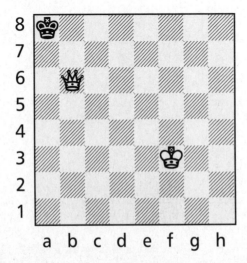

◀ Black to move. Stalemate.

With the King's Help

Now add the strong king, and the stalemating opportunities go up!
Here are a few, with Black to move. They are all stalemate.

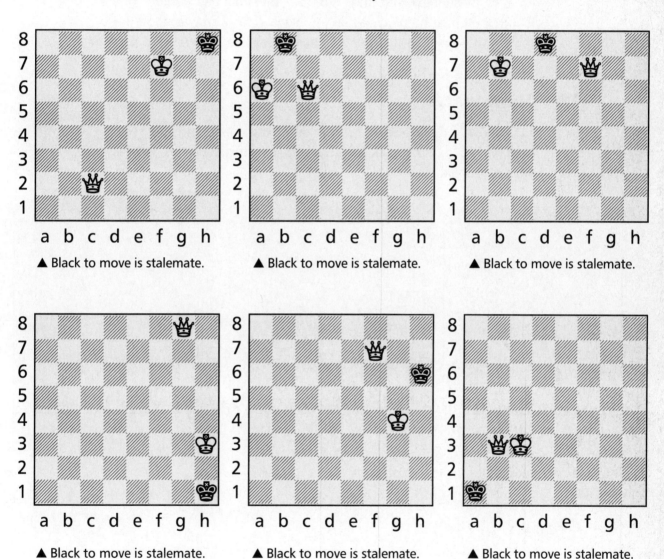

▲ Black to move is stalemate.

▲ Black to move is stalemate.

▲ Black to move is stalemate.

▲ Black to move is stalemate.

▲ Black to move is stalemate.

▲ Black to move is stalemate.

So how can you avoid those nasty stalemates? The best way to make sure you avoid stalemating a lone king is to be aware of the traps and look for them before making your move. Another way of avoiding these traps is to make sure the lone king has a spare square if you don't plan on placing him in check. A third way to avoid these traps is to remember that the queen is a long-range piece, and keep her far away.

The Checkmates

There are more possible checkmates with queen and king versus lone king to go along with the added stalemate possibilities. Here is what they look like:

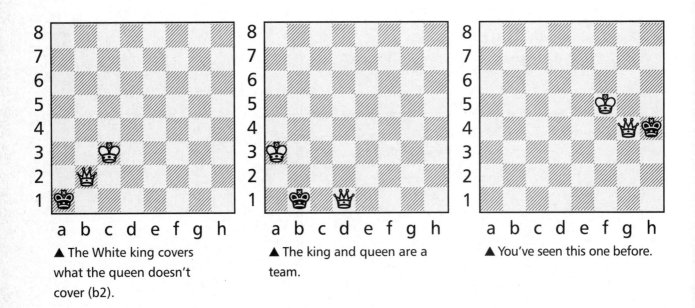

▲ The White king covers what the queen doesn't cover (b2).

▲ The king and queen are a team.

▲ You've seen this one before.

The plan is very much like the one you used with king and rook, except you can dispense with some parts of it. You still have to use the king as a helper, but you don't always need to keep the opposition.

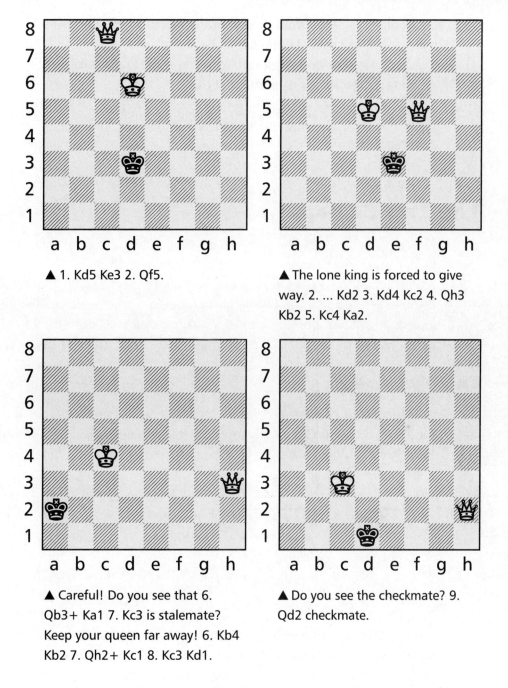

▲ 1. Kd5 Ke3 2. Qf5.

▲ The lone king is forced to give way. 2. ... Kd2 3. Kd4 Kc2 4. Qh3 Kb2 5. Kc4 Ka2.

▲ Careful! Do you see that 6. Qb3+ Ka1 7. Kc3 is stalemate? Keep your queen far away! 6. Kb4 Kb2 7. Qh2+ Kc1 8. Kc3 Kd1.

▲ Do you see the checkmate? 9. Qd2 checkmate.

Practice these king and major piece against king checkmates against your computer or a willing partner. Once you know them cold you can go into a position, even quite a complicated position, in which you have an extra pawn, and you already know a good plan of action:

Step 1: Exchange off all the pieces.

Step 2: Push your extra pawn through to promotion.

Step 3: Use your king and new queen (or rook) to checkmate the lone king.

The Two Bishops

Checkmate can always be forced with king and major piece against lone king. Checkmate can never even come about with king and minor piece against lone king. But with king and two minor pieces against lone king, the situation is more complicated. The plan in all the basic positions involving two minor pieces and king against king is to drive the lone king into a corner of the board. Getting him to the edge just isn't enough.

The Checkmate

The easiest checkmate to get with king and two minor pieces versus lone king is the one in which your two minor pieces are both bishops. Here you can checkmate the lone king in any corner of the board. The checkmates look like this:

◀ The e5-bishop delivers the check and covers g7. The d5-bishop takes away g8. The king takes away g7 and h7.

The plan in these endings is basically simple. Step 1 is to drive the lone king to the corner with the use of both your bishops and your king to methodically take squares away from him. Step 2 is to make sure your bishops have enough room to operate. Step 3 is to get your king out of their way at the last minute.

Working It Out

Although the concept is simple enough, it is very tricky to use the three pieces together as a team. The bishop's power is more subtle than that of the major pieces. Just try to checkmate a lone king using two bishops like you did with two rooks, and you will soon see that it can't be done. So we will look at a checkmate using two bishops and king versus king and work it out, move by move, to understand how it was done.

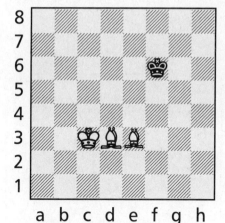

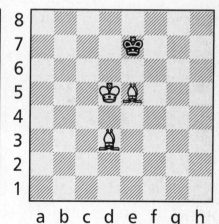

▲ White to move. 1. Bf4. Notice that the fifth rank is off limits to the lone king, thanks to the bishops. 1. ... Ke6 2. Kd4.

▲ The strong king comes up to help. Notice that d6 is off limits to Black. 2. ... Kd7 3. Kd5. Now the sixth rank and c7 are off limits. 3. ... Ke7 4. Be5.

▲ The f6-escape square is taken away. 4. ... Kd7 5. Bf5+. Now much of the seventh rank is denied Black. 5. ... Ke7 6. Kc6.

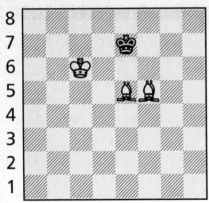

▲ The bishops are perfectly placed, so White now brings his king closer. 6. ... Kf7 7. Kd7 Kg8.

▲ Alert! The Black king can only move to f7 or f8. Therefore White will blow it by moving 8. Ke8 or 8. Ke7, both of which produce stalemate. 8. Ke6. Now Black has a square to go to: f8. 8. ... Kf8 9. Bg6. White takes e8 away. 9. ... Kg8.

▲ This is another alert. The Black king has only f8 as an escape. Therefore, White must avoid 10. Ke7 stalemate. 10. Kf6 Kf8. If Black plays 10. ... Kh8 we end it early with 11. Kf7 checkmate.

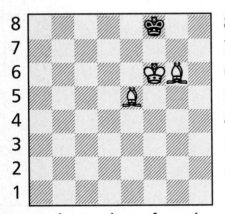

▲ 11. Bd6+ White drives the lone king to the corner. 11. ... Kg8 12. Be4. White gives himself some breathing room while not allowing the Black king out of his box. 12. ... Kh8.

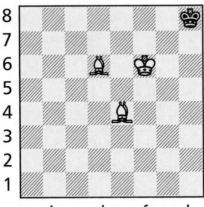

▲ 13. Kg6. The White king makes room for the bishops. 13. ... Kg8 14. Bd5+ Kh8.

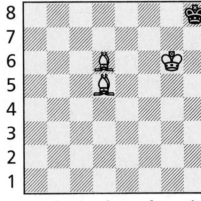

▲ 15. Be5 checkmate.

Learning these king and two minor pieces versus king checkmates is a very good course in learning basic chess strategy. All the principles you have learned and will learn in the future apply: Control the center, coordinate your pieces, use all the pieces, and make use of threats. Once you know these basic checkmates by heart, you will probably already be a pretty good chess player.

Bishop and Knight

This one is the hardest of the basic checkmates. That's because it is no longer good enough to force the lone king into a corner: it has to be the corner of the color of your bishop. You simply cannot produce a checkmate anywhere else.

The Checkmate

The checkmates can take several forms. Here they are:

▲ The bishop delivers the check. Knight and king act in supporting roles.

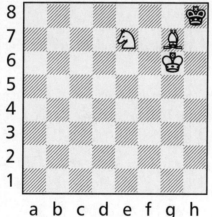

▲ The bishop delivers the check. Knight and king act in supporting roles.

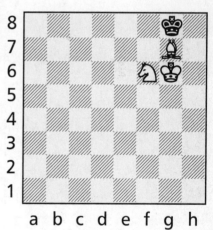

▲ The knight delivers the check. Bishop and king act in supporting roles.

Driving the King

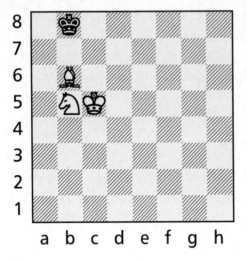

◀ Here is a position well along the way to completion. You will notice that the lone king is very close to the wrong corner.

Phase one of this very complex checkmate is to drive the lone king to the edge of the board. In the diagram, that phase has already been completed. Phase two is to drive the king toward the more friendly corner, and it is done like this:

1. Kc6.

White confines the Black monarch to the eighth rank.

1. ... Ka8.

If Black wants to cooperate with 1. ... Kc8 then White takes the b8-square away with 2. Ba7. But not 2. Bc7 stalemate!

2. Nc7+.

This move drives the king out of his comfy corner. Another stalemate is produced by 2. Bc7.

2. ... Kb8 3. Bc5.

A big key to chess strategy is to not give anything up if you can help it. White keeps all the squares she has gained and prepares to take more away from Black.

3. ... Kc8 4. Ba7.

Now we have the lone king traveling in the right direction.

4. ... Kd8 5. Nd5.

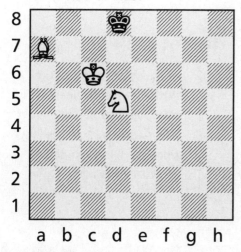

◄ Notice how all the White pieces cooperate in the effort to keep Black from gaining squares.

5. ... Kc8.

Black tries to stay near his most comfortable corner. If he tries to go to the middle, he will wind up in the wrong corner: 5. ... Ke8 6. Kd6 Kf7 7. Bf2 Kg6 8. Ke5 Kg5 9. Nf6 Kg6 10. Ke6 Kg5 11. Bg3 Kg6 12. Bf4. White keeps using all 3 pieces to gradually take squares away from the slippery Black monarch.

6. Ne7+ Kd8 7. Kd6 Ke8 8. Ke6 Kd8 9. Bb6+ Ke8 10. Nf5 Kf8.

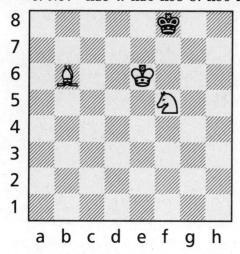

◄ Now White should transfer the bishop to a more useful diagonal.

11. Bd8 Ke8 12. Bf6 Kf8 13. Be7+ Kg8.

Black could end it prematurely with 13. ... Ke8 14. Nd6 checkmate.

14. Kf6 Kh7 15. Kf7 Kh8.

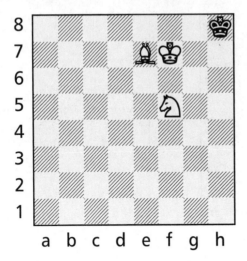

◀ This is a tricky situation. Although the Black king is in the proper corner, it's premature to try to cash in, since there is no good follow-up after 16. Bf6+ Kh7.

16. Kg6 Kg8.

Now we're ready for the final blow.

17. Nh6+ Kh8 18. Bf6 checkmate.

The Two Knights

This one is not possible except against a cooperative opponent. There simply is no way to force checkmate against a lone king when you have king and two knights. Incredible but true.

The only way to convince yourself of the truth of this statement is to try to do it. Any opponent who doesn't wish to get checkmated can simply head his king to the corner. There will always be a way out.

Other Checkmates

The basic checkmates are only a beginning. There are many, many checkmates possible. There are hundreds of them, thousands of them. Although it is impossible to go into detail on all the possible checkmates, not to mention the plans leading up to them, in an introductory work (or, for that matter, in a huge encyclopedic work!), here is a smattering of various checkmates and a little on their history.

Arabian Mate

◄ A rook supported by a knight on the edge of the board cooperate in an Arabian mate.

This one is named after the early Arabian form of the game, before the queen and bishop had their new powers. Thus the strongest pieces in use were the rook and knight. The rook always produces this mate, and is defended by the knight, which also covers the king's escape square.

Epaulette Mate

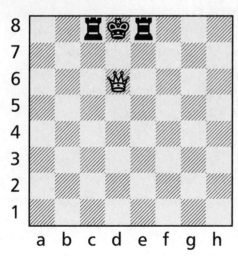

◄ The king wears these fringes in the form of his own pieces or pawns, which take away his escape squares on either side.

Gueridon Mate

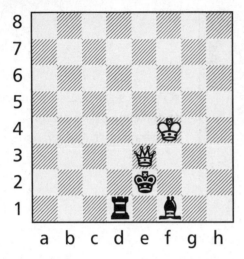

◀ A *gueridon* is a small French café table. The king represents the tabletop, while the pieces or pawns diagonally behind him, which deny him those squares for escape, represent the table legs.

Anastasia's Mate

◀ Anastasia's mate is actually a special corridor or back rank mate, with a rook delivering the mate and the escape squares taken up by a friendly pawn and an enemy knight.

This one is named after *Anastasia und das Schachspiel*, an 1803 novel by Wilhelm Heinse.

Philidor's Legacy

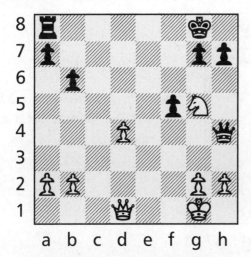

◀ All the ingredients are here for a Philidor's Legacy Mate.

The ingredients include the open b3-g8 diagonal, a White queen able to get there with check, an exposed Black king on g8 with Black pawns on g7 and h7, the White knight on g5, a Black rook guarding the eighth rank, and complete White control over the f7-square. This is a form of smothered mate that Philidor first worked out in the eighteenth century. It goes like this:

1. Qb3+ Kh8.

If 1. ... Kf8. White plays 2. Qf7 mate.

2. Nf7+ Kg8.

Note that the Black king and the White queen are on the same diagonal. The only reason there isn't a check is that the White knight is in the way on the same diagonal. So White moves it out of the way with:

Setting up the enemy king for destruction by forcing his own pieces to take away his escape squares is a worthy goal. The sacrifice of the queen makes it appear spectacular, but the idea of setting up a smothered mate as in Philidor's legacy is actually quite logical.

3. Nh6+.

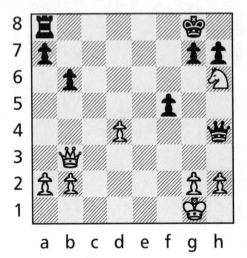

◀ A double check is extremely powerful. The only way out is to move the king.

3. ... Kh8.
Now what?

4. Qg8+!!

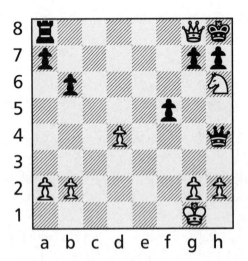

◀ There is only one way to get out of check. Black must capture the rude intruder with his rook.

4. ... Rxg8 5. Nf7 mate.

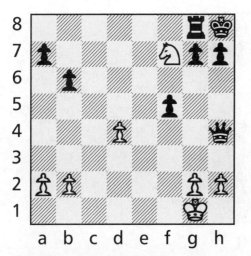

◄ The end result of a Philidor's Legacy Mate is always a smothered mate.

Who needs the queen when you have a knight that can do such great work?

Smothered Mate with Pin

This one comes right out of the opening. In it, the White king is caught in the middle, surrounded by his own pieces and pawns. It goes like this:

1. d4 Nf6 2. c4 e5 3. dxe5 Ng4 4. Bf4 Bb4+ 5. Nd2 Nc6 6. Ngf3 Qe7 7. a3 Ncxe5.

◄ Should White capture the bishop?

8. axb4 Nd3 mate.

◄ Looks like he should have left the bishop alone and defended his king instead!

The e2-pawn cannot capture the checking knight because that would expose the White king to the baleful eye of the Black queen. Ⓔ

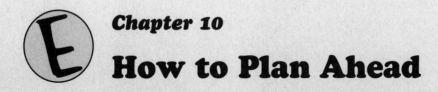

Chapter 10

How to Plan Ahead

Throughout most of a game, you cannot reasonably plan a checkmate. So what is left to plan? You can plan to specifically improve your position within the next couple of moves, or you can come up with a general theme you want to promote. The former is referred to as *tactics*, and the latter is referred to as *strategy*.

Tactics

These short-term plans can encompass anything that will help you to improve your position or anything that will interfere with your opponent's position. When you bring a new piece into play—controlling a center square and preparing to castle, for instance—that is part of your tactical plan. (Castling itself can often fit in well with such short-term goals. It helps to bring your rook to the middle while helping to hide your king away behind a wall of pawns.)

FACT

Long-range, general goals for the future are *strategic plans*. They include gaining control of key squares, creating and pushing a passed pawn, using all your pieces, and exposing your opponent's king. More immediate goals of improving your position and/or destroying your opponent's position are *tactics*. These include various forms of double attack and any immediate threat.

Building for the Future

These kinds of moves just referred to are tactical because they offer immediate improvement of your position. You will need to be careful in determining where to place your pieces, though, since you do want them to be available later in the game. So placing a piece in the center where it will immediately perish is generally not a good idea.

You have to see far enough ahead on each move to know whether your move is safe. Am I placing the piece en prise? Will my opponent be able to attack this piece in the next couple of moves? Am I leaving anything open to attack by moving this piece? These are the kinds of questions you must answer before deciding on a particular move.

Threats

The general idea of what tactics is all about centers on immediate threats. You threaten a checkmate or to capture a piece, and your opponent responds with a threat to capture one of your pieces or to checkmate your king. These threats can take many forms, as you learned in Chapter 8 and will learn more about in the next chapter.

The threat to capture pieces, often combined with actual captures, is the most appealing and also the most difficult part of tactics. You absolutely have to be aware of all threats as well as the consequences of them all in order to be able to play a strong game.

FACT

A combination is a planned series of tactical moves using captures, checks, and threats of all sorts to gain an advantage or wipe out a disadvantage. Most combinations involve at least a temporary sacrifice of some sort, giving up something of importance in order to reap the rewards a little later.

Planning a tactical sequence of moves involves seeing ahead several moves. But more importantly, it involves judging the consequences of the sequence. For instance, consider the following position.

◀ With Black to move, the first thing that should spring to mind is that White threatens to invade on f7, capturing a pawn with either bishop or knight.

You can try various defenses, such as 1. ... Nh6, 1. ... Be6, 1. ... Qe7, and 1. ... Bxe5. Look at them all and assess the consequences.

1. Nh6 brings a new piece into play, but doesn't attempt to control central squares. Further, are you ready to meet 2. Bxh6 in a way that both recaptures the piece and saves the f7-pawn?

1. ... Be6 goes for the center and even threatens to capture the White

bishop. But are you ready to answer 2. Bxe6 with 2. ... fxe6, exposing your king and ruining your pawns?

1. ... Qe7 doesn't really defend the pawn at all. White plays 2. Nxf7, picking off the pawn clean, and even getting the rook in the corner.

But 1. ... Bxe5 saves the pawn while getting rid of that annoying knight. White can threaten the pawn again along with checkmate by playing 2. Qh5, but 2. ... Qe7 seems to defend everything adequately while bringing another piece into play.

Strategy

Long-range plans may involve some immediate threats as an incidental part of the strategy, but mostly we are looking at a general buildup over many moves. These long-range plans can also be looked at as threats, but the immediacy of tactical threats is missing, so strategic threats are subtler.

Types of Plans

Of course the ultimate idea behind all plans is to eventually get a checkmate, or at least to avoid getting checkmated. But a plan to checkmate can be successful only if there is some way to get at the opposing king. Against an experienced opponent, that sort of situation isn't easy to set up. So during most of the game, you will be working with more modest goals.

FACT

There are literally hundreds of books on strategy and planning in chess that are available in your local library or through the USCF or the Internet. Chess magazines of all types usually have a section or several articles devoted to this very important aspect of the game. Even computers are getting into the act, with software available that teaches how to form and carry out a game plan.

A typical early strategic plan is to bring out all your pieces in order to control the center. Once you have accomplished that, the next stage might be to force a breach in your opponent's pawns or to get a bishop pair on an open board working against two knights or a bishop and a knight. Or you might work to create a passed pawn or to get a powerful knight posted in your opponent's territory. Another strategic goal could be to double up your rooks on a file in order to penetrate into your opponent's half of the board. Or it could be simply to expose the enemy king to an attack.

Carrying out the Plan

Once you get the hang of forming strategic plans, your only trouble will be carrying them out. The problem is that your opponent probably doesn't want you to carry out your plan, so will try to stop you. It's something like deciding to walk to the corner store in an unfriendly neighborhood or in the middle of a blizzard. You can do it, but it requires courage, persistence, and preparation.

When you have the advantage, you must attack, or you will lose your advantage. But beware of two things: First, make sure you really have a big advantage. Second, make sure you can find a way to continue the attack. Otherwise, your advantage can disappear through timidity or poor tactics.

Your strategic plans have to be realistic, or you'll never be able to carry them out. At the same time, plans that are too modest won't get you very far either, even if you do carry them out. For instance, if you plan to draw your game, the trouble is that you just might succeed. In such a case you never had a chance to win because you never tried.

Seeing Ahead

All plans, whether short-term or long-term, require that you see into the future at least a bit. You have to be able to predict what the chances of success will be with any given plan. With a combination, as long as it isn't too complex, you can often see right through to the end of the captures and threats. Then it's a matter of counting up what is left and assessing the results. A strategic plan is often harder to see through to conclusion before you begin because there are so many things that can go wrong when you don't account for specifics.

A great way to carry out a strategic theme is to use threats and combinations to back up your theme. The following game fragment is a case in point:

1. d4 d5 2. c4 dxc4 3. Nf3 c5 4. e3 a6 5. Bxc4 b5

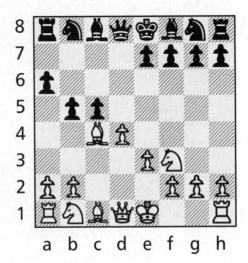

◀ Position after 5. ... b5.

White has completed the first part of his plan from the beginning. He has developed bishop and knight aggressively and controls the center. Meanwhile, Black has only moved pawns. Not a single Black piece is moved yet.

But White is confronted with a dilemma. His bishop is under attack. What to do? It feels wrong to retreat the bishop when White has the only pieces in play and controls the center. The strategic plan demands an attack.

So common sense and tactics come to the aid of strategy. White controls the a2-g8 diagonal. Black's king is the only defender of his f7-pawn, which is on that diagonal. The a8-h1 diagonal also beckons, since Black has an undefended rook sitting there at a8, and White has a queen ready to go to f3. There is a very nice, strong central outpost for White's knight on e5.

Can we make use of all these features of the position? Yes, we can, with the following combination: **6. Bxf7+**. White sacrifices bishop for pawn with the idea of bringing the Black king out into the open, vulnerable to a White knight on e5 and a White queen on f3.

6. ... Kxf7 7. Ne5+ Ke8 8. Qf3.

◄ White threatens checkmate on f7 and the en prise a8-rook. One of them will have to go.

8. ... Nf6 9. Qxa8.

And White has won the Exchange for a pawn, and exposed the Black king as well.

Another way to carry out the same idea is with a different move order: 6. Ne5. White threatens 7. Bxf7 checkmate.

6. ... bxc4 7. Qf3

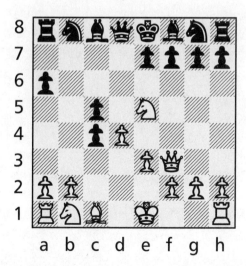

◄ Now White threatens 8. Qxf7 checkmate as well as the en prise rook.

7. ... Nf6 8. Qxa8.
And White has won the Exchange.

What if my opponent doesn't go along with my plan?
If your plan is good, this shouldn't matter. A good plan takes all reasonable moves and plans into account. If your opponent tries something unreasonable, chances are it will be bad, and he just did you a favor. But if his move is both good and unexpected, you should take time out to reassess the situation. You might also have resources that you didn't foresee.

Planning Greater Force

A frequent strategic plan is to win material. This comes in different forms, ranging from winning a free pawn to winning the Exchange to promoting a pawn and thus all of a sudden going up a whole queen. This kind of plan will only work under the right conditions, however. And such plans often run the risk of allowing your opponent a different kind of advantage, such as giving her more squares or a good attacking position.

Conditions for Winning Material

In order to have a reasonable amount of success with a plan of winning material you have to have some idea of what material you are going to win. And that material must be weakened in some way. The material you're after should meet one or more of the following conditions. It should be:

- Underdefended
- Undefended
- Exposed
- Too far away
- Unable to move

Under those conditions, you should have a reasonable chance of winning the desired material.

In the last example, the a8-rook was undefended and exposed, so it should not be surprising that White was able to plan for its capture.

What Are You Giving Up?

This one is harder to judge. Again in the last example, Black tried to win the White bishop. The problem with his plan was that it succeeded! His win of the bishop ultimately cost him his king's safety, the center, and his poor exposed rook.

There are pieces and pawns left unattended every day that are best left alone. One example should suffice:

1. d4 Nf6 2. c4 e5 3. dxe5 Ng4 4. Bf4 Nc6 5. Nf3 Bb4+ 6. Nbd2 Qe7.

◀ Position after 6. ... Qe7.

Black has been bringing out new pieces with every turn, focusing on the e5-pawn, and is now poised to win it. This will recover the pawn he sacrificed back on move two. White decides to mess up the Black plan by threatening to capture the bishop on b4, which certainly seems like a reasonable thing to do.

7. a3 Ncxe5.

But Black leaves the bishop en prise and recovers his pawn instead. Does this make sense? He could have played 7. ... Bxd2+ easily enough, after all.

8. axb4.

◀ White believes that Black simply overlooked that the bishop was en prise. But it was White who overlooked something important. What did White fail to note?

8. ... Nd3 checkmate.

He was not aware that his king had no possible moves, or perhaps he was unacquainted with this particular checkmate. What a harsh way to find out!

Traps introduced by seemingly absurd giveaways lurk everywhere in the game of chess. Yet you can't simply avoid capturing anything that is offered. Such an attitude is far too timid, and won't help win games. The best way to solve this dilemma is to look all gift horses in the mouth before deciding whether or not to make the capture. Analyze the consequences of each and every capture, and you will go a long way toward playing a strong chess game.

Controlling the Center

Here is a plan that both players strive for from the very beginning. At least, they do if they are experienced players. So how can you wrest the center away from someone who is trying as hard as you are for its control?

The simple answer is to focus all your resources on controlling those essential squares. While planning to win material, while planning an attack on the king, while planning to bring all your pieces into the game, while keeping a sharp eye out for tactical opportunities, don't forget to focus all your moves on the center.

There is more than one way to go about controlling the center. In fact, there are essentially two ways to go about such control: You can strive for the classical pawn center or you can try for the hypermodern center.

The Classical Pawn Center

This approach boils down to "put your pawns in the center and keep them there." At the end of the nineteenth century, the chess giant and first world champion Wilhelm Steinitz promoted this kind of a center, and at the turn of the twentieth century, the famous chess teacher and author Siegbert Tarrasch codified the idea. Tarrasch went so far as to suggest that without a strong pawn center your game will likely collapse.

The idea is simple enough. Since pawns are the least powerful of the chess family, place them side by side in the center and you deny any central squares to your opponent's pieces.

A great example of fighting for central control with pawns is the following opening variation:

1. e4 c6 2. d3 d5 3. Nd2 e5 4. Ngf3.

Black has more pawns in the center than White does, but White has more pieces in play. White also threatens to win the e5-pawn.

4. ... Nd7 5. d4.

◀ Position after 5. d4.

White once again threatens to win the e5-pawn, and he still has more pieces in play. And notice that both sides have filled up the entire center with pawns.

The Hypermodern Center

This is an idea that had always been known, but wasn't often used early in the game. It is really a counterattacking idea. The so-called *hypermoderns* decided that a big, fat pawn center can make a great target for an attack by the pieces. So they came up with ways to avoid putting pawns in the center. Instead, they set up their positions to attack their opponent's pawns, which were obligingly always there in the center.

FACT

Hypermodern was a slightly derogatory term when it was first used, after World War I. It was put on chess players and theoreticians who decided that the old classical ways were suspect. There was quite a debate about whether or not the hypermoderns were right. Their ideas became accepted as an alternative method of fighting for the center.

Getting All Your Pieces Involved

This is another plan that every good player uses. It is sometimes difficult to understand how you can get all the pieces into the game when you can move only one with each move. But patience, good judgment, and a sharp eye for tactics will make this plan readily available.

The following game, which you've already seen (in Chapter 6), is a model of developing every piece purposefully. Watch how White brings new pieces into play using threats at nearly every turn. Those few moves when a new piece is not brought into play involve capturing and threatening to capture. (White: Paul Morphy; Black: Duke and Count; Paris, 1857.)

1. e4 e5 2. Nf3.
A new piece comes to the center, threatening the e5-pawn.

2. ... d6 3. d4.
Lines are opened for the queen and the c1-bishop, while there is a threat to the e5-pawn.

3. ... Bg4 4. dxe5.
This move opens up the d-file for the queen and grabs a pawn.

4. ... Bxf3 5. Qxf3.

This recovers the piece, saves the queen, and gets the queen into the action.

5. ... dxe5 6. Bc4.

A new piece comes into play with a checkmate threat on f7. Kingside castling is also prepared.

6. ... Nf6 7. Qb3.

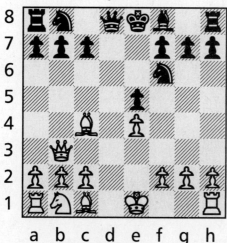

◀ This transfer of an already developed piece comes with two threats: one to the underdefended f7-pawn and the other to the undefended b7-pawn.

7. ... Qe7 8. Nc3.

A new piece comes into play, defending the e4-pawn.

8. ... c6 9. Bg5.

A new piece comes into play, preparing queenside castling.

9. ... b5 10. Nxb5.

The bishop is saved at the cost of the knight. White will get two pawns for the knight along with an enduring attack on the uncastled Black king.

10. ... cxb5 11. Bxb5+.

The bishop comes into even more powerful play, checking and getting the second pawn.

11. ... Nbd7 12. 0-0-0.

The king gets tucked safely away while the rook commands the d-file.

12. ... Rd8 13. Rxd7.

This move serves to expose the enemy king while making room on d1 for the other rook.

13. ... Rxd7 14. Rd1.

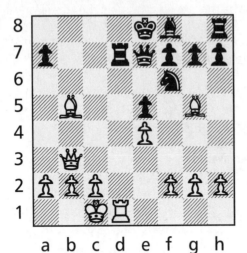

◄ White gets the last piece into play, threatening a destructive exchange on d7.

14. ... Qe6 15. Bxd7+.

This move captures the rook and checks the king, while making extra room on the b-file for the queen.

15. ... Nxd7 16. Qb8+.

This check gives up the queen but forces Black to open the d-file for the White rook.

16. ... Nxb8 17. Rd8 checkmate.

◄ With this checkmate, White has used every piece to its maximum potential.

Develop New Pieces

Developing a new piece with each turn as far as possible is essential to good chess play. Here is an example of what happens when one player heeds this advice and the other player doesn't:

1. e4 c5 2. d4 cxd4 3. c3 dxc3.

White is playing a gambit, in which he gives up a pawn in order to bring more pieces into the center quickly.

4. Nxc3 Nc6 5. Bc4 Nf6 6. Nf3 d6.

◄ White's queen and bishop command nice open lines, while he also has more pieces in play.

7. e5! Nxe5.

Black avoids the horrors of 7. ... dxe5 8. Qxd8+ Nxd8 9. Nb5 Rb8 10. Nxe5, but what he gets is worse.

8. Nxe5 dxe5 9. Bxf7+ Kxf7 10. Qxd8.

Exposing the King

This is always a good plan to have, provided you have a means of carrying it out. An exposed king can easily get checkmated, while one well shielded is harder to get at.

Consider this famous example. (White: Edward Lasker; Black: Sir George Thomas; London Chess Club, 1912.)

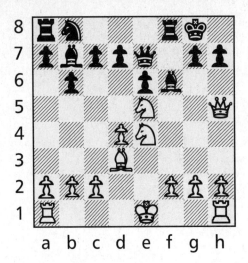

◀ White to play. Notice before we begin the final assault that White controls the center and has four pieces in play pointed at the Black king. Winning combinations do not spring out of random positions.

1. Qxh7+!! Kxh7.

The king comes out into the open. Of course, he has no choice in the matter.

2. Nxf6+ Kh6.

Or 2. ... Kh8 3. Ng6 mate. White continues to play forcing moves, keeping the Black king in check. While flying from each check, Black never has time to protect his king or win the game with his extra queen.

3. Neg4+ Kg5 4. h4+ Kf4 5. g3+ Kf3 6. Be2+ Kg2 7. Rh2+ Kg1 8. Kd2 mate!

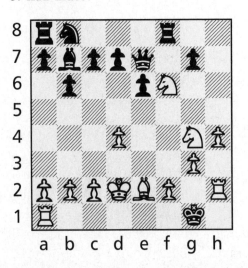

◀ The Black king has taken a strange journey to meet his demise.

The chess world is filled with combinations in which one player sacrifices his pieces in order to bring the opponent's king out into the open, where he will be vulnerable to an early checkmate. Those that work are often very beautiful and make the archives. Those that fall short serve as warnings that such attacks need to be accurately calculated.

Planning Defense

Defense is often harder to plan that an attack because it requires you to find a potential attack to defend against. And nobody wants to contemplate the various ways in which an opponent can destroy your position.

Nevertheless, it pays off to sniff out potential attacks on your position. If you make ready for the enemy attack, it probably won't overwhelm you. So here are three good defensive plans you can use when weathering a storm.

- Trade pieces.
- Bring up extra defenders.
- Have a good attack.

Trade Pieces

When there are too many enemy pieces swarming about your king, get rid of some of them. Trading your opponent's attacking pieces is one of the best ways to stop her attack. Here is an example:

1. e4 e5 2. Nf3 Nc6 3. d4 exd4 4. Bc4.
White has given up a pawn to get more pieces into play.

4. ... Bc5 5. Ng5.
White now attacks the f7-square, but fails to get a new piece into play.

5. ... Nh6 6. Qh5 Qe7.

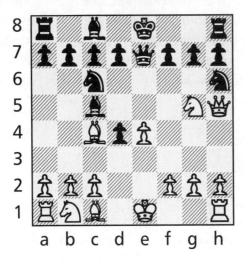

◀ White now recovers his pawn, but he has to trade two pieces in order to do it, and that breaks the attack.

7. Bxf7+ Nxf7 8. Nxf7 Qxf7 9. Qxc5 d6.

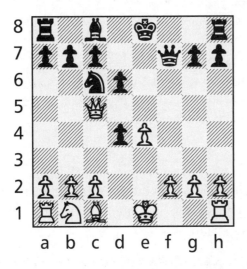

◀ White has no attack. In fact, Black is attacking the lone White piece that's in play and is getting ready to bring still more pieces into play himself.

The greatest defenders could also wield powerful attacks. How could it be otherwise? In order to be able to put up a good defense, you have to be able to see the opponent's attack coming many moves in advance, perhaps before your opponent spies it! And if you can see attacks developing that far in advance, you will certainly be able to produce a few good attacks yourself.

Bring up Extra Defenders

This is often a good way to put down a building attack. It stands to reason: You don't try to make a basket in basketball with a two-on-five break. That's backward. So if you surround your king with many defenders, he will be very difficult to get at.

Here is an example:

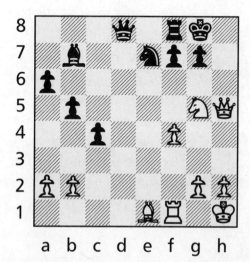

◀ Black to move. White threatens checkmate on h7.

Black needs extra defenders, so he looks at 1. ... Be4. Since this loses the bishop, he has to try something else. Then he finds **1. ... Qd3!**, which adds an extra defender to h7 while threatening checkmate on f1.

2. Kg1 Qg6.

◀ Black is ready to trade White's attacking queen for his own defender.

Have a Good Attack

An old sports saying that has a lot to recommend it is "The best defense is a good attack." This often applies in chess as well. Take a look at the following famous combination played by Adolf Anderssen against Lionel Kieseritzky in 1851 (ever since dubbed the immortal game).

◄ White to move. White controls the center and has more pieces in play—by a lot! So instead of defending the en prise rook he builds up the attack.

18. Bd6! Qxa1+ 19. Ke2 Bxg1.

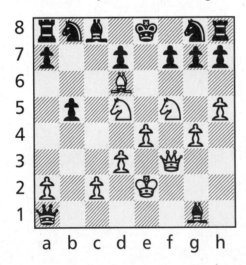

◄ Now White is out of rooks, but still has four pieces on the attack while Black didn't bring out any more pieces or bring more defenders to his king.

20. e5 Na6 21. Nxg7+ Kd8.

◄ White now forces checkmate in two moves.

22. Qf6+! Nxf6 23. Be7 checkmate.

When defending by attacking, it is essential that you make sure what you are going after is worth what you are giving up. It does no good to defend an attack on your queen by attacking an enemy rook, unless there is more to your attack. Checkmating attacks, threats to promote a pawn or two, and massive buildup of your attacking force are often worth a lot. When it comes to defending against an attack on one piece by attacking another, usually the deciding factor is what other aspects of the positions change, such as the control of the center or who has more pieces in play. Ⓔ

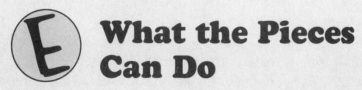

Chapter 11

What the Pieces Can Do

It's time to learn a bit more about what the pieces can do. Some of these special tactics can be executed by a single piece, while some can be pulled off only with a combination of pieces. The special tactics you are about to learn include double attack, fork, discovered attack, pin, and skewer.

Double Attack

There are special tactics that involve a double attack. The idea is simple: Attack one piece and your opponent will probably be able to defend it or move it easily enough. But when you attack more than one piece, your opponent has to stretch his resources, finding a way to cover everything that is under attack. That can be much more challenging than taking care of one problem at a time.

So how can you attack more than one piece at the same time? You can move only one piece at a time, after all. Actually there are various ways to do this. They are based on the principle of making full use of your pieces.

Fork

This is the easiest of the double attacks to understand. One piece attacks two or more, making use of its potential. Every piece is capable of delivering a forking attack, and even the lowly pawn can pull this one off.

In each example, you will see the position before the fork and the position after the fork. For convenience, a Black piece will do all the forking attacks in each set of positions.

Perhaps you will be surprised to know that the king can also execute a fork. But why not? The king can move in many different directions, after all. It's just necessary to slip him in between two enemies by attacking their weak spots. That is, attack them where they cannot strike back.

FACT

There can be many prongs in a fork. A pawn can threaten to capture two pieces while threatening to march up a square to promote, making three prongs. A queen or knight can menace up to seven enemies at once!

Queen Fork

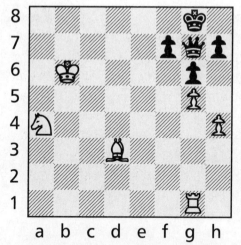

▲ Black has the chance for a five-pronged fork: 1. ... Qd4+.

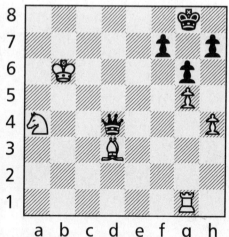

▲ The queen threatens rook, bishop, knight, and pawn along with the check. After White gets out of check, with, say, 2. Nc5, Black will play 2. ... Qxg1.

Rook Fork

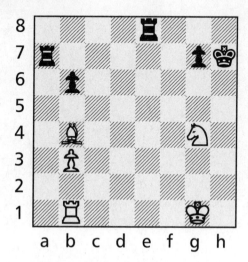

▲ None of the White pieces is defended. Why not attack as many as you can? Black plays 1. ... Re4.

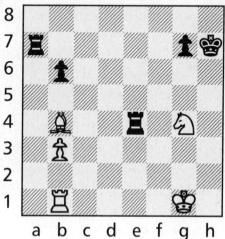

▲ White will either lose the bishop or the knight. He cannot save both.

Bishop Fork

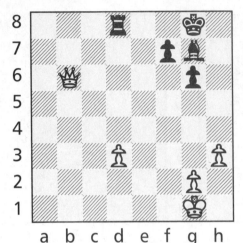

▲ Although the Black rook is en prise to the White queen, Black sees a great chance. He defends the rook by attacking with 1. ... Bd4+.

▲ The Black bishop forks the White king and queen. All White can do is get something for the queen with 2. Qxd4 Rxd4.

Knight Fork

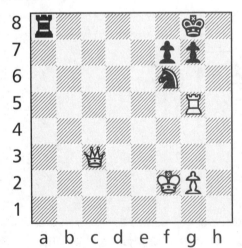

▲ Black has a fabulous move available here. It is called a *family fork*, since Black attacks practically the whole family at once: king, queen, and rook.

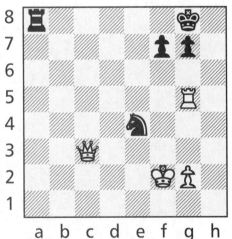

▲ White must move the king, whereupon Black pockets the queen.

King Fork

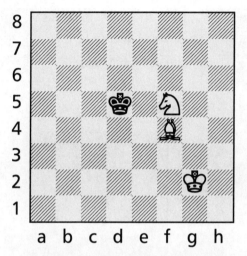 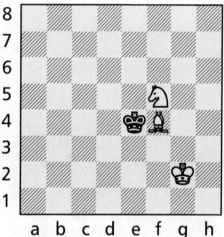

▲ This would normally be a White win, but it is Black's move, and he strikes out powerfully with the fork 1. ... Ke4.

▲ White cannot save both pieces, so must lose one and with it all checkmating opportunities.

Pawn Fork

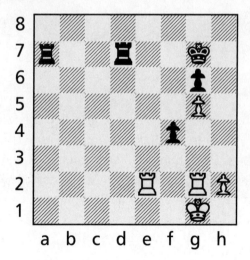 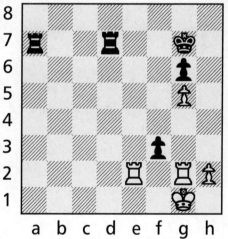

▲ The White rooks are positioned just right for Black, who plays 1. ... f3.

▲ Black gets one of the White rooks.

Center Fork Trick

One of the best-known combinations in the early part of the game is the center fork trick. In it, Black temporarily gives up a piece in order to regain it later with additional central control and open lines to bring out the rest of his pieces:

1. e4 e5 2. Nf3 Nc6 3. Bc4 Nf6 4. Nc3.

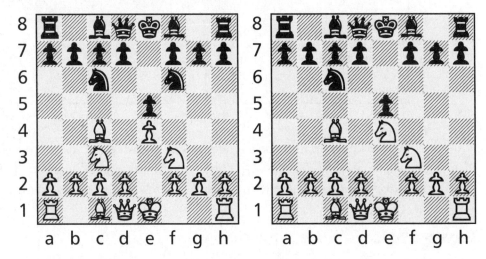

▲ Here is where Black gives up the piece: 4. ... Nxe4 5. Nxe4.

▲ And here is where he regains it with the center fork trick: 5. ... d5.

Discovered Attack

This one is more complicated. It requires a player to use two friendly pieces on the same move. The way to do that is to make use of the long-range power of queen, rook, or bishop. This long-range piece is masked by almost anything at all—king, pawn, knight, rook, or bishop—and the masking piece moves out of the way.

> As long as there is an enemy piece or pawn on the line that contains the long-range piece and the masking piece, we have a discovered attack.

The Attacking Piece

This is the essence of a long-range piece's attacking power. The piece sits in an unobtrusive, out-of-the-way place, and radiates power outward. In order for a discovered attack to function, one of these pieces has to be lined up with another friendly piece in front of it, and an enemy piece further along the same line.

Here are examples of discovered attacks about to happen, using each of the long-range pieces. White moves in each case.

Queen:

◀ White plays 1. Nf6, attacking knight and queen.

Rook:

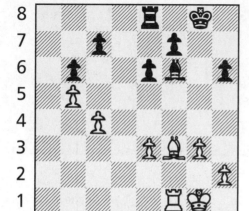

◀ White plays 1. Bc6, attacking rook and bishop.

Bishop:

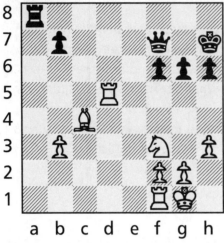

◀ White plays 1. Rd8!. The enemy pieces that are attacked can strike back by capturing one of the attacking pieces. But Black loses the queen or the rook no matter how the play goes.

The Masking Piece

This can be any piece except a queen—even a king or a pawn. As long as it has the power to get out of the way, you've got the ingredients for a discovered attack.

In the examples you just saw, a knight, bishop, and rook were used as masking pieces. Here are two more examples where a king and pawn are used as the masking piece that gets out of the way. It is White to move.

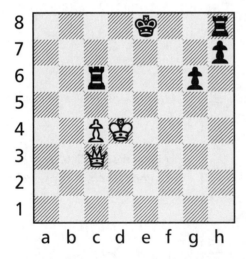

▲ White plays 1. Kd5 and both rooks are en prise.

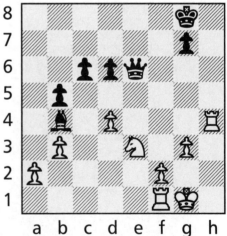

▲ After 1. d5, White is attacking the queen, c-6 pawn, and bishop for a triple attack.

The Enemy Piece

There is no discovered attack if there is nothing to attack. So the third ingredient for a successful discovered attack is the enemy piece. Of course, the more powerful or important the enemy piece, the better it is. In the examples, we saw enemy queens, rooks, bishops, knights, and even a pawn attacked by way of a discovered attack.

This last ingredient is really what makes discovered attacks so strong and hard to defend. In each of the cases we looked at, the discovered attack was particularly effective because both White pieces were threatening to capture something.

FACT

It is possible to play a discovered attack where only the long-range piece being uncovered is the one attacking anything. But it's generally much more effective if the unmasking piece can also attack something.

The idea behind the discovered attack is just plain good chess. It pays to know it well. Here is a trap that shows how important such knowledge is:

1. d4 d5 2. c4 e6 3. Nc3 c6 4. Nf3 f5 5. Qc2 Nf6 6. Bg5 Bd6 7. Bxf6 Qxf6 8. cxd5 cxd5.

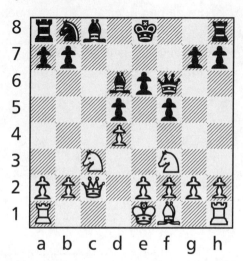

◀ White spies his queen and the c8-bishop on the same c-file. Only his knight is in the way. So how to take advantage of the situation? With the discovered attack 9. Nxd5!

Discovered Defense

This idea is less well known, but is still important. It can be used to defend all sorts of things while continuing with a plan of development and center control when something is being attacked. Here is a sample of discovered defense in action:

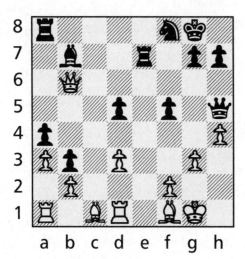

◄ White to move doesn't want to move the en prise d1-rook since there's nowhere good to put it. But he can let the a1-rook do the defending and even threaten something himself with 1. Bg5.

Discovered Check

This is nothing more than a special form of discovered attack. The reason this move is special lies in the piece under attack. It happens to be the enemy king; thus it results in a check. Since checks are so important, this is one of your most effective tools in a chess game. The check comes from seemingly nowhere, since the piece you move does not do the checking.

Examples of Discovered Check

Here are a couple of wonderful examples of discovered check.

1. e4 e5 2. Nf3 Nf6 3. Nxe5 d6 4. Nf3 Nxe4 5. d4 Bg4 6. h3 Bh5 7. Qd3 Qe7.

◀ Alarm bells should go off in White's head. The Black queen is on the same file as his king! But White sees a fork that comes with a check, and so lacks a proper sense of danger.

8. Qb5+.

Here it is: a three-pronged fork on the Black king, b7-pawn, and h5-bishop.

8. ... c6.

This little pawn move threatens the queen, gets out of check, and defends the b7-pawn with a discovered defense. Of course, the bishop on h5 is still en prise. But it's nothing more than juicy bait.

9. Qxh5.

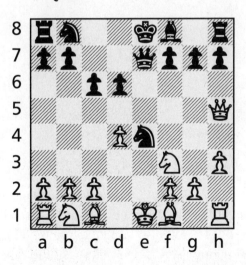

◀ There is a surprise in store for White, whose king and enemy queen are on the same e-file, along with an enemy knight.

9. ... Nf6+.

This discovered check takes White by complete surprise. The knight does the moving, threatening the White queen along the way. But it is the Black queen that does the checking.

You may be wondering if the shielding piece can deliver a check. Of course! Any piece or pawn can deliver a check at any time during a game, provided the enemy king is within range. Discovered check refers to a situation where the long-range piece is "discovered" giving check after the shielding piece moves out of the way. But the shielding piece can deliver check in an otherwise normal discovered attack. Here is an example with White to move:

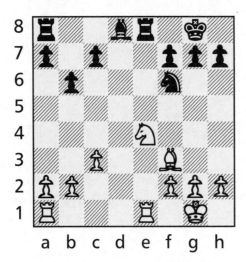

◀ White wins the Exchange with the discovered attack 1. Nxf6+.

The discovered attack is on the rook, and the shielding piece is giving check.

1. ... Bxf6 2. Bxa8 Rxa8.

Double Check

Since either piece can deliver check in a double attack, one wonders whether both can do so at the same time. And in fact they can. This little bit of overkill is known as a *double check*.

When both pieces deliver check at the same time, the enemy is placed in an immediate quandary. Just think back to the three possible ways out of check. In a double check you cannot block the check, since you will be blocking only one of the two checks. You also can't capture the checking piece, unless you do so with the king itself, since otherwise the other checking piece would still be checking. The only way to defend against a double check is to move the king! Thus a double check often has devastating power.

Here are some examples of that most powerful weapon, the double check.

1. d4 d5 2. c4 c6 3. Nc3 Nf6 4. Nf3 Bg4 5. Ne5 Bf5 6. g3 Nbd7 7. Bg2 e6 8. 0–0 Nxe5 9. dxe5 Nd7 10. cxd5 exd5 11. e4 dxe4 12. g4 Bg6 13. Nxe4 Nxe5 14. Bf4 Nd3 15. Qe2.

◀ White sets up a double check that is most efficient.

If Black takes the bait with 15. ... Nxf4 we get 16. Nf6 checkmate. This is a checkmate even though both checking pieces are en prise. Remarkable! Furthermore, if Black wants to wait a move to take the bait, we get 15. ... Bxe4 16. Bxe4 Nxf4 17. Bxc6 checkmate.

◀ This is another checkmate while both checking pieces remain en prise.

Pin

This is a weapon that requires two enemy pieces on the same line with a friendly long-range piece. Instead of two good guys and one bad guy on the line, as in a discovered attack, we have one good guy holding two bad guys hostage. Well, only one of them is actually held hostage, but they both have to be there.

The pin is more akin to a wrestling pin than to a sewing pin. In it, one friendly long-range piece looks at a powerful enemy piece with a less powerful enemy piece shielding it.

The Pinned Piece

This is the lesser enemy piece that acts as a shield to the more powerful or more important enemy. Some really good examples of pinned pieces come up in the Morphy versus Duke and Count game from 1857 that you saw back in Chapter 6 and again in Chapter 10. Here it is again with the pins pointed out:

1. e4 e5 2. Nf3 d6 3. d4 Bg4.

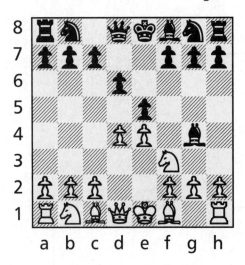

◀ The White knight is pinned to the queen.

4. dxe5 Bxf3 5. Qxf3.
Now there is no more pin.

5. ... dxe5 6. Bc4 Nf6 7. Qb3 Qe7 8. Nc3 c6 9. Bg5.

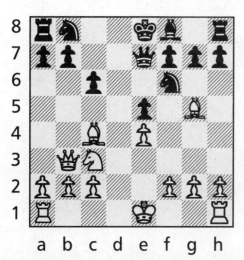

◀ The Black knight is pinned to the queen. This pin stays around for a while.

9. ... b5 10. Nxb5 cxb5 11. Bxb5+ Nbd7.

◀ The Black knight is pinned to the king.

12. 0-0-0 Rd8 13. Rxd7 Rxd7.

◀ Now it is the rook that is pinned to the king.

14. **Rd1 Qe6 15. Bxd7+ Nxd7 16. Qb8+ Nxb8 17. Rd8 checkmate.**

Absolute Pin

On move eleven of the game you just looked at, Black moves a knight into the way of the checking bishop and the king. This blocks the check, so is good. But it also puts Black into an absolute pin. That is, a pin in which the pinned piece (the knight on d7) not only shouldn't move, but can't move.

One of the best ways to take advantage of a pinned piece is to hit it again and again. If you want to break down your opponent's defenses, harsh measures are called for. So when you spy an immobile piece, such as a pinned piece, attack it again. This is much more effective than simply exchanging the pinning piece for the pinned piece.

Whenever a piece lies between your king and an enemy long-range piece, it is in an absolute pin. It cannot move out of the line of fire, since you are not allowed to place your king in check.

Skewer

A skewer, sometimes referred to as an *x-ray attack*, is sort of a mirror-image pin. It requires a long-range piece and two enemy pieces on the same line of attack, just like a pin does, but in a skewer the more important or powerful piece is doing the shielding. Therefore, instead of immobilizing the piece, a skewer practically forces it to move, thus exposing the poor little guy it had shielded. When the two enemy pieces are of the same value, it is also referred to as a *skewer*, rather than a pin.

FACT

Pins and skewers are nothing more than specialized forms of double attack. It's just that both enemy pieces stand on the same line, so the attacking is being done through one piece on to the other.

Here is an example of a skewer in action:

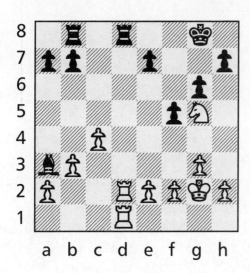

◀ This position, with Black to move, came up at a regional tournament in the Midwest during the mid-1990s.

The player handling the Black pieces didn't notice a short combination leading to a skewer, and so failed to defeat the chess master he was playing.

First, notice that White threatens to win a rook, since he has a battery of rooks on the d-file. Black can move his rook out of the way with 1. ... Rdc8 or exchange rooks. Here's what happens if he exchanges rooks:

1. ... Rxd2 2. Rxd2

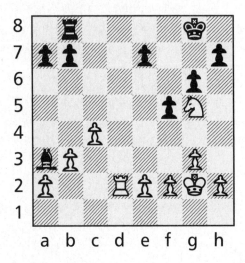

◀ Do you see the skewer now? Simply look for any two White pieces on the same line as one of your long-range pieces (you've only got two), and you will see it.

2. ... Bc1!

Here it is. The rook is more powerful that the knight. If it moves out of the way, Black will simply capture the knight:

3. Rd7 Bxg5.

The best defense is to let the rook go with 3. Nf3. That way, White at least gets the bishop for the rook after 3. ... Bxd2 4. Nxd2.

FACT

There are many kinds of tactical setups that require more than two pieces. These include convergence and batteries (two friendly pieces going after an enemy), discovered attacks of various sorts (two friendly pieces going after more than one enemy), forks (one piece going after more than one enemy), and pins and skewers (one piece going after two enemies). These are part of your arsenal of weapons in chess.

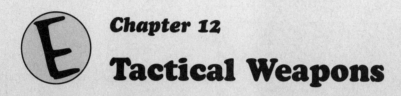

Chapter 12

Tactical Weapons

Besides the various sorts of double attack, there are other tactical things the pieces can do. These include, but are not limited to, removing the defender, overload, interference, Zwischenzug, desperado, and no retreat. These ideas can take place using various units of attack and defense. All are based on very sensible attacking ideas that every chess player should know.

Removing the Defender

The idea behind removing the defender is simply to get rid of the support a piece has. You remember that one of the five ways to meet a threat to capture is to defend the threatened piece. Well, this tactic gets rid of that defender.

1. e4 e5 2. Nf3 Nc6 3. Bb5 Nf6 4. d3 a6

◀ The e5-pawn is under attack by the knight on f3. It is also defended by the knight on c6. So White removes the defender and picks up the pawn for free one move later.

5. Bxc6 dxc6 6. Nxe5.

Here's one a bit more complicated.

1. e4 e5 2. Nf3 Nc6 3. Bb5 d6 4. d4 Bd7 5. Nc3 Nge7 6. Bc4 exd4 7. Nxd4 g6 8. Bg5 Bg7.

◀ Black threatens to capture the knight on d4. He has a converging attack with his knight on c6 and bishop on g7, while White only defends with his queen.

9. Nd5.

White did not defend the d4-knight. What does that mean? Black decided to find out the hard way.

9. ... Bxd4.

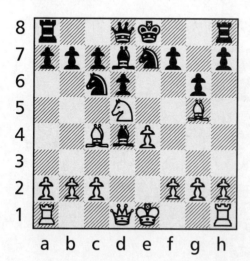

◄ White's knight went to d5 so it could get to f6 with a check. But f6 is defended—by the bishop on d4. Therefore, White removes it.

10. Qxd4! Nxd4.

So what did White get for his queen? How about a checkmate?

11. Nf6+ Kf8 12. Bh6 checkmate.

All these tactics, whether long-range or short-range, are possible with the right buildup. It is merely necessary to know what you are looking for and then find a way to implement it.

The hard part is that you have an opponent who doesn't want you to pull off any of those tricks. So you need to learn to look at whatever position is in front of you with a keen eye for any of the patterns you have learned. When one begins to take shape, play for it. The rewards will come soon enough.

Overload

A related concept to removing the defender is the overloaded piece. In this one, a piece is doing more than its fair share, and an astute opponent notices this and takes advantage of it.

1. e4 c5 2. Nf3 d6 3. g3 Nc6 4. Bg2 Bg4 5. 0–0 Nd4 6. h3.

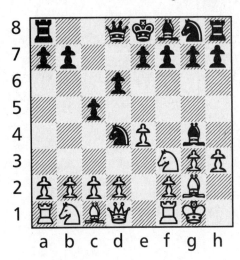

◀ The g2-bishop is doing double duty. It is defending both the pinned knight on f3 and the pawn on h3.

Black makes use of this situation to win a pawn.

6. ... Nxf3+ 7. Bxf3 Bxh3

QUESTION?

Why are queens less than ideal defenders?
The queen is powerful. She can defend as well as attack. But using such a valuable resource as a backup for stray pieces and pawns detracts from her attacking power. She can quickly become overloaded when spread too thin.

Interference

Another type of overloading is shown through the subtle idea of interference. In this one, a piece gets in the way or interferes with two cooperating pieces. It is White to move.

◀ First the king is driven back so he can interfere with the Black rooks defending each other: 1. Rh7+ Ke8.

Next the White queen swoops in to get at everybody: **2. Qe6+ Kd8 3. Qd6+.**

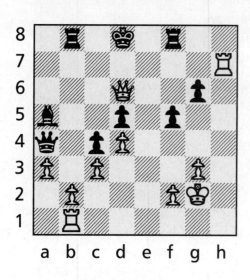

◀ We have a tragic-comic situation. The rooks can defend each other as long as the Black king doesn't interfere. But there's no way for him to slip out, and one of the rooks will exit as a result of the queen's triple fork.

3. ... Kc8 4. Qxf8+.
White has picked up one of the rooks.

Zwischenzug

This one isn't as difficult as it may look or sound (the Zs are pronounced *ts*). As explained in Chapter 8, *Zwischenzug* is a German word meaning "in-between move." It refers to a situation where one player responds to a threat by ignoring it temporarily in order to threaten something else that is more important. After the more important threat is seen to, the player may come back and take care of the original threat.

More often than not, a Zwischenzug is a check or an attack on the queen. These are threats not easily ignored. Here is an example that happens very early:

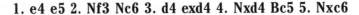

1. e4 e5 2. Nf3 Nc6 3. d4 exd4 4. Nxd4 Bc5 5. Nxc6

◀ Black does not have to recapture the knight right away. Instead, he can play the Zwischenzug 5. ... Qf6, which threatens checkmate.

Only after White has seen to the checkmate threat with, say, 6. Qe2 will Black recapture the knight.

The early play you have been witnessing is called the *opening*. Openings are a series of moves by both players that bring about a position each is comfortable with. Chess masters have been playing and compiling openings for hundreds of years, and there are not too many positions you can reach early in the game that some master hasn't at least experimented with at some time or other.

The following opening trap is very interesting because it contains several Zwischenzugs.

1. e4 e5 2. d4 exd4 3. Qxd4 Nf6 4. Bg5 Be7 5. e5.

◀ Black doesn't move the f6-knight, which is under attack, relying instead on a Zwischenzug.

5. ... Nc6!

◀ Black expects White to move his attacked queen.

But moving the queen causes trouble. For instance, 6. Qc3 loses to the pin 6. ... Bb4, while 6. Qe3 runs into the fork and discovered attack 6. ... Ng4. So, rather than defending the queen, White plays his own Zwischenzug.

6. exf6! Nxd4 7. fxe7.

And White gets the queen back after all. But just who profited the most from this series is not quite clear.

ALERT!

A Zwischenzug is simply carrying out the old sports adage "the best defense is a good attack." Always remember to take a further look at whatever threats are looming after a Zwischenzug, or, as in the previous example, a series of Zwischenzugs. Just make sure you always are aware of each and every threat to check or capture at all times during a game.

Desperado

This tactic is named after the bad guys in the old Westerns. When you're going to lose a piece in any case, take something out with it. When you think about it, this is nothing more than plain common sense.

1. e4 e5 2. f4 Bc5 3. Nf3 Nc6 4. Bc4 d6 5. c3 Bg4.

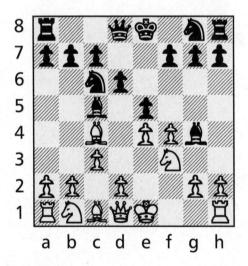

◄ White spies a chance to win a pawn using a discovered attack. But has she looked far enough ahead?

6. Bxf7+ Kxf7 7. Ng5+.

◀ Here is the discovered attack. The pin is broken and the Black king is in check. Therefore, White will get back her bishop. Except for the desperado.

7. ... Qxg5!

Black sees that moving the king will result in losing the bishop. If the bishop is going to be lost, why not take something out with it? Like a knight? If the queens get exchanged after 8. fxg5 Bxd1 9. Kxd1, Black winds up with an extra piece. The same thing happens if White tries a Zwischenzug with 8. Qb3+ Be6.

◀ If White tries her own desperado with 9. Qxe6+ Kxe6 10. fxg5, Black always winds up with an extra piece.

The reason is that he started the combination up a piece to begin with, and captured a second piece right at the start. All White could do was recover one of her pieces here with 9. Qxb7 Qd8 10. Qxc6 Qe8.

No Retreat

When a piece has nowhere to move, simply threaten to capture it. This one is often the cause of a desperado. So make sure when you trap a piece that can't move safely that it really can't move safely!

A famous opening trap involves trapping a bishop that has no retreat. It goes like this:

1. e4 e5 2. Nf3 Nc6 3. Bb5 a6 4. Ba4 Nf6 5. 0–0 Be7 6. Re1 b5 7. Bb3 d6 8. d4 exd4 9. Nxd4 Nxd4 10. Qxd4 c5 11. Qc3 c4.

◀ As you can see, the White bishop has nowhere safe to move. The desperado 12. Bxc4 bxc4 13. Qxc4 doesn't give White enough for the piece.

This trap is so old it's affectionately referred to as the *Noah's Ark trap*. So if you fall for it, you're in good company.

No retreat means no forward moves as well. When the situation comes up, the piece in question simply has nowhere safe to move.

ALERT!

No retreat means a piece is all dressed up with nowhere to go. Any piece that has no safe moves is vulnerable to attack. Make sure your pieces have an emergency exit.

◀ White to move. Where can the queen go safely?

Here is an example of a queen that has no retreat. She actually has lots of legal moves forward, backward, and sideways; it's just that each and every one of them will get her captured. That's no retreat. Ⓔ

Chapter 13

Putting It All Together

As a review of what you have learned you will look at the following game, played between a master and an expert (the rating class just below master). Throughout the game there are many of the tactics you have learned. The players also make use of the strategy you have learned, developing pieces and playing to control the center.

Time or Force?

This game has as its main theme a rather continuous struggle between time and force. Time means what is happening right now: it refers to the immediate threats that have to be met one way or another immediately. Force refers to the amount and type of pieces and pawns the players have to deal with.

The Initiative

Each player sacrificed some material in order to gain the initiative. The key questions to ask when confronted with such possibilities are "How much material am I giving up?" (which is best answered by a detailed calculation of the forcing moves, to make sure you don't lose more than you intend), and "How long will my initiative last?"

FACT

The initiative is an ongoing situation during a game. One of the players keeps making threats, thus forcing the game into channels of his choosing. When you have the initiative, you decide where and when the play takes place. This is a powerful weapon when used with authority.

The latter question is often hard to answer exactly, but if you have more pieces in play *after* the combination, and they can continue to make threats, while your opponent has difficulty getting his pieces into play, you can often justify a fairly substantial investment of material.

The Game

Get out a set and board, or even two sets and boards if you have them. It is possible to follow a game like this through in your head, but you will miss a lot if you are not very experienced. (White: Master; Black: Expert; Los Angeles, 1981.)

The Opening

1. e4 g6

The game opens up a little differently than you have seen. White puts a pawn in the center while Black prepared to fianchetto his bishop, striking at the center through the flank. This is one of the hypermodern openings.

FACT

Openings are divided up into five general categories: 1. e4 e5; 1. e4 something else; 1. d4 d5; 1. d4 something else; and 1. something else. These categories are rather wide, and there is sometimes some overlap. In the current game we begin with 1. e4 something else, but later Black plays ... e7-e5, so it's not entirely clear in which category this opening belongs.

2. d4 Bg7 3. Nc3 d6 4. Nf3 Nf6 5. Be2 0–0 6. 0–0.

Both players have been developing pieces and focusing on king safety and the center. White has an extra piece in play and an extra center pawn, but of course it is Black's move. The opening has turned into the Pirc Defense, which is named after Vasja Pirc, a twentieth-century Yugoslavian grandmaster.

6. ... c6.

Black opens a diagonal for his queen and fights for control of the central square d5.

7. h3.

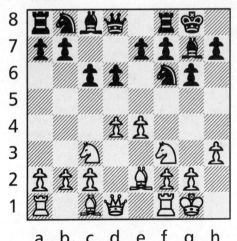

◀ White makes sure the f3-knight will not get pinned.

So far the players have been careful with each other. Nothing very exciting has happened, but each player has been building up a solid position, hoping to be ready for the threats when they come.

The Threats Begin

7. ... e5!?

Black is making sure he has his fair share of the center. But isn't this move a mistake? Black must know there are two White forces converging on e5, while he has only one pawn defending. Shouldn't White simply win the pawn?

8. dxe5 dxe5.

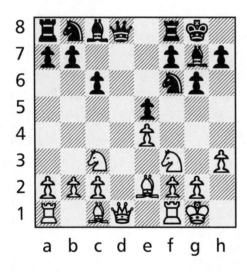

◄ White to move.

9. Qxd8.

Recognizing and using threats are the hallmarks of a strong chess player. If you do not disrupt your opponent's plans forcefully with threats, she will most likely carry them out.

Discovered Attack

Trying to win the pawn directly with 9. Nxe5 won't work because of the discovered attack 9. ... Nxe4! 10. Nxe4 Bxe5. So White exchanges queens in order to pull the f8-rook away from the defense of its king.

9. ... Rxd8.

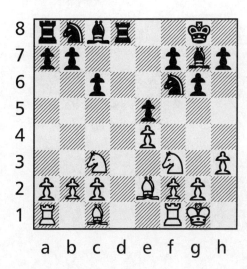

◀ White to move.

10. Bc4.

This move threatens 11. Nxe5, with an attack on the vulnerable f7-square. The alternative 10. Nxe5 still does not win a pawn because of a series of desperados.

Discovered attacks are some of the most insidious weapons in chess. The piece that moves may capture something and/or threaten something. But that is all gravy. The unmasked piece and its threat are what weak players will not notice.

Desperado

10. Nxe5 is the attempt to win a pawn. It is answered by the discovered attack 10. ... Nxe4, which regains the pawn. Now White can try the desperado 11. Nxf7. White will lose this knight anyway, so he picks up a pawn with his dying breath.

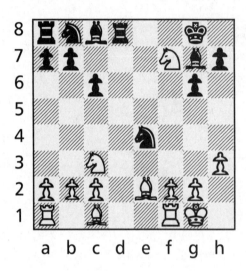

◀ Black's d8-rook and e4-knight are en prise.

But Black has his own desperado: With 11. ... Nxc3 Black also sells his knight, but picks up a piece on the way. In this position, if White should capture the knight, Black will also capture a knight. So best is 12. Nxd8 Nxe2+ and you can see that Black has come out ahead in this desperado tradeoff. He has two minor pieces for a rook and pawn, a slight material advantage. The combination has turned out to Black's advantage.

FACT

Figuring out who gets the better of a series of desperado captures can be very confusing. Try to follow the series through in your head and count up the pieces at its end. If there is more than one variation, you have to do the same with each one and compare the final positions in each. No wonder chess can take a lifetime to master, though it can be learned in a mere half-hour!

Missed Opportunity

Back to the position after Black's ninth move:

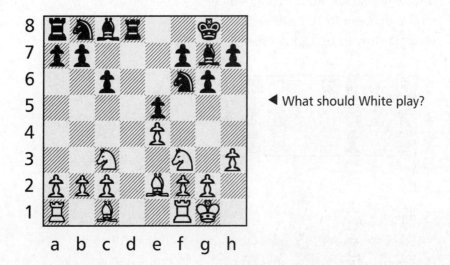

◀ What should White play?

It turns out that White missed an opportunity. It's true, he can't win a pawn, but he can get a lead in development with 10. Nxe5 Nxe4 11. Nxe4 Bxe5 12. Bg5 Re8 13. Rad1.

Opportunities abound throughout any chess game. The strong players are the ones who recognize and pounce on these opportunities more often. Some opportunities aren't always easy to find, for they require subtle thought and understanding, or they require you to look quite deeply into the position.

FACT

All the opportunities were not taken advantage of in this game between a master and an expert. This is understandable, and quite usual. Even the world's strongest grandmasters miss opportunities, though not as many. And when they do miss out, the opportunities are usually of a more subtle or deeper variety.

So we return to the game, where White has just played 10. Bc4.

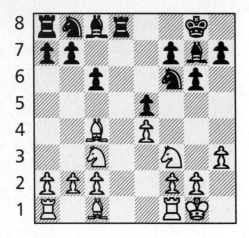

◀ Black to move.

a b c d e f g h

10. ... b5.

After this move, White is committed to the sacrifice of a piece. The reason the continuation in the game is forced is because alternatives are so bad. To put the bishop on d3 now would be to admit the whole idea beginning with 8. dxe5 was mistaken. The bishop would be passively placed, and Black would take over the initiative.

11. Bb3 b4.

ALERT!

Opportunities abound in practically all chess games. Therefore be on the alert at all times. You never know when your chance will come.

Forming a Plan

There really is no longer a choice. Saving the knight will just drop the e-pawn for nothing. But White was expecting this since playing 10. Bc4. The whole idea of exchanging pawns on e5 and then queens on d8 was to soften up the f7-square so this bishop and a knight could converge on that sensitive square.

12. Nxe5!

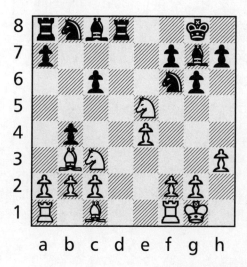

◄ White has voluntarily given up his knight. He will get three pawns and the initiative for it.

This piece sacrifice is very easy to evaluate. White is castled, controls the center, and is slightly ahead in development. In addition, White will get three pawns for the piece, and the combination is the most forcing continuation. It is also the only way to carry out the plan begun on the eighth move.

Whether White or Black is better after the combination is irrelevant. If White is worse, then the plan beginning on the eighth move was wrong. This logical follow-up is the only chance at this point.

Taking the Bait

12. ... bxc3.

Black did not have to capture the piece. An alternative is to simply get the pawn back by catching up in development with 12. ... Be6 13. Bxe6 fxe6 14. Ne2 Nxe4 15. Nc4.

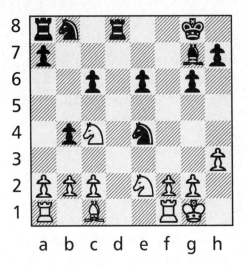

◀ If Black doesn't take the gift knight, he gets a playable game.

This is quite a reasonable alternative. But of course White has a better position, since the Black pawns are scattered. In any case, Black wants more than a reasonable alternative. He wants to win the piece.

Discovered Check

13. Nxf7.

◀ This move sets up a discovered check. The threat is simply to capture the rook, delivering check at the same time.

13. ... Rf8 14. Nd6+ Kh8 15. bxc3.
White gets the third pawn for his sacrificed knight.

◀ The natural culmination of White's piece sacrifice.

Evaluation

It wasn't too hard to foresee this position, even as far back as the eleventh move. Three pawns for the piece, a powerful, passed e-pawn, the possible check on f7 at any time, the open a3-f8 diagonal for the dark-square bishop, the central files for the rooks, and Black's backward queenside development all point to an excellent game for White.

But Black does have an extra piece. This means White will have to be very accurate in his attack. Any little slip could give Black the advantage very easily.

15. ... Ba6.

Black continues to develop pieces. He does so with a gain of time as well, since this move threatens to win the Exchange.

◀ White to move. What would you do?

A Slip

16. Rd1.

Where should White put the rook? Does it belong on the open d-file or does it need to back up the passed pawn from e1? White makes the wrong choice because of being overly concerned about having his rooks on e1 and a1 with a possible Black bishop coming to c3. But that will never happen if the e4-pawn marches to e5!

Correct is 16. Re1! Rooks belong behind passed pawns! After that, 16. ... Nfd7 17. Bd2 gives White a powerful center and a big advantage.

The move played is a case of the wrong rook going to the right square. After this mistake, Black takes over the initiative, sacrificing the Exchange to do so.

Everybody makes mistakes, even very strong players. When you notice that something has gone wrong, keep your head. Assess the position and make new plans. It will not help to berate yourself or become discouraged during a game.

16. ... Nbd7 17. Ba3.

◀ The a3-bishop and f8-rook are now on the same diagonal, with only a White knight in the way.

You cannot carry out any tactical plan without carefully preparing for it. The position in front of you may contain hints of what to look for, but you have to be able to interpret those hints.

Set Up

White sets up a discovered attack by bringing this bishop in line with the Black rook shielded by a knight that can move with check. Discovered attacks don't happen by themselves: They have to be set up.

17. ... h6.

Black gives his king a better square to go to than g8, which is exposed to the White b3-bishop.

18. Nf7+.

The Initiative

18. ... Rxf7!

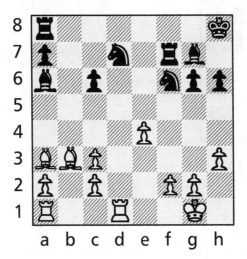

◄ Black's surprising Exchange sacrifice, which nets the White e-pawn, turns the game around.

By playing this way, Black takes control of the game. Notice how he makes threats with each move, and wins the e-pawn as material compensation for the Exchange.

Energetic play, comprised of strategic and tactical threats, is the hallmark of good chess players. Black takes over the initiative with this Exchange sacrifice, and keeps it for a while.

19. Bxf7.

Fork

19. ... Ne5!

Black plays a centralizing move which threatens the en prise bishop, while defending the g-pawn. This is a form of the fork just like discovered defense is a form of discovered attack. The object of every attack doesn't always have to be the opponent's forces. It can sometimes be a key square or something of yours that needs defending.

20. Bb3 Nxe4.

◀ Black controls the center and his pieces are active.

Black picks up the key central pawn while threatening to capture another pawn on c3. Note the latent power of the bishop on g7. Some discovered attacks are getting ready to happen. In the meantime, White is starting to have troubles. Just look at that Black center. It's very powerful.

21. Bb4.

Convergence

21. ... Nc4.

Black again threatens to capture on c3. White not only needs to find a way to stop this threat, though. He also needs to find a way to stop Black from making threats with every move.

In order to break the opponent's initiative, you will often have to ignore whatever horrors he is hammering you with and give back some of what you are getting. Make your own threats, so that the other guy has to choose between carrying out his threats and meeting your threats.

Counterattack

White needs to choose how to handle the position. Defend with 22. Rd3 or counterattack?

◀ White to move. What would you do?

22. Rd7.

This choice is aggressive but chancy. White decides to abandon the c3-pawn. Instead of defending it, he brings his pieces into Black's territory. This is often a practical way to steal the initiative against an opponent who has been pounding away at your position.

A Variation

Here's a look at what could happen with the defensive move:

22. Rd3 c5. Of course Black could move his knight with a discovered attack on the rook. But since the knight can't threaten anything by moving, that allows the simple Re3. So Black threatens to win the bishop. 23. Re1. White meets Black's threat to his bishop with a threat to the Black knight, incidentally getting his last piece into play. 23. ... Ncd2. Finally Black plays the discovered attack. 24. Rxd2. And White gives back the Exchange in order to break the Black initiative. 24. ... Nxd2 25. Bxc5 Bxc3 26. Re7.

◀ With the converging attack on a7, White will get the third pawn for his piece again.

a b c d e f g h

Rooks can be very strong on the seventh rank (or second rank if it is a Black rook). Anything on the seventh rank is not defended by a pawn. Thus it is often desirable to get rooks into enemy territory.

Back to the Game

◀ It is Black to play after 22. Rd7. He has the initiative. How can he keep it?

a b c d e f g h

22. ... Nxc3.

Black in his turn finally captures the pawn, setting up a discovered attack on the long dark diagonal. But by doing so, he lets the initiative slip out of his grasp. In fact, this powerful-looking capture turns out to be the losing move.

Another Variation

So what should Black play? Why, he should ignore any White threats and make more of his own! 22. ... c5 does the job quite nicely. The pawn on c3 and the bishop on b4 both hang. Here is a sample of what could then happen:

23. Bxc4.
White gives the bishop on b4 somewhere to go.

23. ... Bxc4 24. Ba3 Nxc3.
Black threatens that discovered attack by checking on e2.

25. Re1.

◀ The fierce fight for the initiative continues in this variation.

White saves the rook and threatens to get a second rook to the seventh rank, which would ruin Black's whole day.

25. ... Ne2+.
This check blocks the e-rook from the seventh rank.

26. Kh1 Re8.
Black now threatens a horrible check on g3 with a discovered attack on the hanging rook.

27. Red1 Bd4.

This is the type of play Black should aim for. With two minor pieces for a rook and pawn, his material advantage isn't much, but his initiative is hard to contain. Lots of pawns are hanging in these positions, but the Black center looks awesome, and his pieces are very active.

QUESTION?

How can I follow separate variations when playing over a game?
A good way is to use two boards and sets to follow the game. Make the actual moves of the game on one board, and go over the variations on the other board.

◀ This is the position in the game after 22. ... Nxc3. White to play. What would you do?

The premature capture on c3 gives White a chance to turn the tide of the game once again. Do you see White's winning combination?

Removing the Defender

23. Rxg7!

This move removes the defender of the knight on c3.

But in this case the theme goes beyond just winning two pieces for a rook. The fianchettoed bishop on g7 was also the pride and joy of Black's game.

This kind of move isn't so hard to find, especially when you can foresee that it doesn't sacrifice material. In fact, it wins material by force! The forcing nature of the combination makes these kinds of moves possible to calculate.

23. ... Ne2+.

Accuracy

24. Kf1!

◀ Although this walks into a possible discovered check later, it is the only way to be certain of getting both minor pieces for the rook. Hiding on h1 or h2 loses more material after 24. ... Kxg7.

FACT

Calculating a series of captures accurately takes practice. That's why one of the best things you can do (if you want to become a strong player) is to try to solve any position you see. Practice on positions that occur in somebody else's game or that you see in a chess book or magazine, with or without a label saying "White to move and win!"

Positional Desperado

24. ... Ng3+

Since Black will lose the knight in any case, he at least doubles up the White pawns which are hiding their king. Thus tactics can be used to do more than win pieces or checkmate. They can also be used to bring about a better position in any number of ways.

25. fxg3 Kxg7 26. Kf2.

◀ The fireworks are over.

Winning a Won Game

So no discovered check happened after all. Now White is a pawn up with the two bishops versus bishop and knight. It should be a matter of technique to win from here, but winning technique in superior positions isn't such an easy prospect. It requires constant vigilance and attention to detail. You do not want to miss a threat at this point.

26. ... Rd8 27. Re1 Rd7.

Black prevents White from getting another rook into his seventh rank. One was enough!

28. Re6.

Since White cannot penetrate to the seventh rank, he penetrates to the sixth rank, where he threatens to win the en prise c-pawn.

28. ... Rf7+ 29. Ke1 Rc7 30. a4.

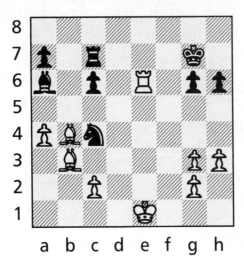

◀ The idea in playing this move is to take away as many squares from the Black knight as possible. The threat is to march the pawn to a5 for that purpose.

Making It Easier

30. ... Kf7.

Black walks into a horrible pin. Notice the bishop on b3. He should try 30. ... Nb6 31. a5 instead.

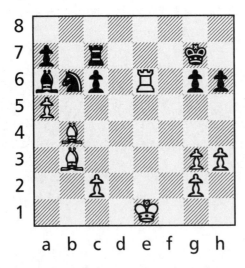

◀ After Black plays the better 30. ... Nb6 and White pushes the knight further back with 31. a5.

31. ... Nc8. This isn't pleasant, but Black stays alive.

Just as bad as the move played is the aggressive-looking blunder 31. ... Bc4, when 32. axb6 Bxb3 33. cxb3 axb6 win's a piece for White.

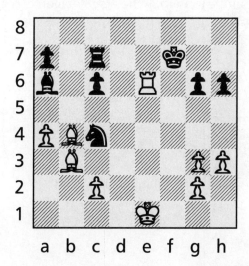

◀ Position after 30. ... Kf7.

Defending a difficult or losing position is a very hard task. And yet, the difficulty isn't so much that it's hard to find good moves. Rather, it's psychological.

Whenever you are in a losing position, something has gone horribly wrong. You certainly didn't plan on getting into this mess! So you get depressed, lose concentration, and make further mistakes.

On the other hand, with the right attitude, defending isn't so hard after all. What more can go wrong? You're already lost. So look around for the best possible move. Resist to the last. That way, an inattentive opponent can chalk up the win in his head while you pull out a stunning defense.

Pin

31. Re4.

This combination, based on the pin along the a2–g8 diagonal, wins two more pawns while getting the rooks off the board. Without it, the game might have dragged on for a very long time.

31. ... c5.

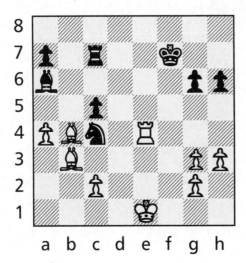

◄ White to play. What would you do?

32. Ba3.

White makes sure of the win. The only way Black can save the piece is to force a trade of rooks, which is just what White wants.

A Variation

White had other ways to play the position. One fails to get the most out of the position because of a Zwischenzug: 32. Bxc4+ Bxc4 33. Rxc4 Re7+. The Zwischenzug. 34. Kd2 cxb4 35. Rxb4. And White didn't trade rooks and is only two pawns up.

The other works out well enough, and would also serve White well. It is based on a temporary pin as well as a Zwischenzug: 32. Rxc4. The c-pawn is temporarily pinned. 32. ... Bxc4 33. Bxc4+. This Zwischenzug saves the other bishop. 33. ... Ke7 34. Bc3. White has two bishops and an extra pawn for the rook.

◀ Black has a trick to save his pinned knight, but it will cost him two pawns. Position after 32. Ba3.

32. ... Re7.

This neat counterpin is the only way for Black to avoid losing a whole piece. Unfortunately for Black, it commits him to a rook exchange, and he loses another pawn at the end of all the captures.

33. Rxe7+ Kxe7 34. Bxc5+ Ke6 35. Bxa7.

◀ With three extra pawns and the bishop pair, White will not have any trouble winning.

Black is now down two pawns, including two passed pawns, and White has the positional advantage of two bishops versus bishop and knight as well. Therefore, Black resigned the game. There is really no point to playing on without any prospects for winning or even somehow grabbing a draw.

ALERT!

The two bishops are a positional advantage against a bishop and a knight or against two knights because they sweep the whole board. Their long-range power is always there, but when you have both of them, they cover all the squares on the board very quickly. Knights can also cover all the squares, but are slower, while a lone bishop can only cover half the squares on the board.

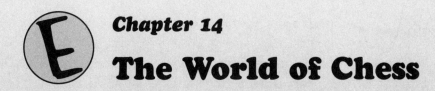

Chapter 14

The World of Chess

Now that you know how to play a reasonable game of chess, some new opportunities are available. There is a whole world built around the subculture that is chess. The following is just a sampling of what this chess world has to offer.

A Parlor Game

Chess is at its core simply a game between two players. A board and set is the only essential equipment, and even that can be dispensed with by those with strong enough imagination and concentration to play blind.

Anywhere

The game can be and is played virtually everywhere. At home, in a restaurant, coffee shop, or bar, in the library, outside in the park, on a train, and in the backseat of a car are a few places where a casual game can take place with no organization whatsoever.

Whether played in private or in public, such games are traditionally referred to as *skittles*. The chief difference between such casual chess and organized tournament games is a lack of time control, a lack of scorekeeping, and the danger of kibitzers.

QUESTION?

What is a *kibitzer*?
Literally an interfering onlooker, kibitzers are spectators who suggest moves to one or both of the contestants. This is illegal in any formal competition, of course, but is often tolerated in casual play. *Kibitzer* is a Yiddish word from the German *Kiebitz*.

The Park

Outdoors there are areas in city parks where chess is played daily, at least in the warmer months. Games can be timed or not, depending on the availability of clocks or the inclination of the players. You can also play for stakes or merely for the sake of playing. Washington Square Park in New York City is famous for this, and was brought to the attention of the general public in the book and movie *Searching for Bobby Fischer*.

Chess Clubs

In between the informal games that anyone can play anywhere and serious tournament competition, there is what used to be the backbone of chess, the chess club.

FACT

In the eighteenth and nineteenth centuries, the Café de la Régence in Paris was a famous meeting place for many of the day's intellectuals, and that included chess players. Other clubs, perhaps of similar type, sprang up around Europe and, later, the United States. Such clubs were gathering places for people of diverse background and interests. They helped provide a common culture for their habitués.

Men's clubs of all types grew out of old-style intellectual gatherings. Eventually, these clubs began to specialize, and clubs devoted entirely to chess gained currency. Even many of those clubs included checkers and/or bridge as activities for a long time.

Club Activities

At a typical chess club, members and guests can find a casual game, or get involved with whatever level of organized competition the club offers. Ladder play, where each member rises or falls in reference to other club members, was always a popular way to keep track of everyone's progress, at least until ratings came into vogue. Besides regular blitz tournaments and the club championship, there is often league play, where each club in an area plays the other clubs throughout the course of a season. (During a blitz tournament, each player gets five minutes to complete all the moves in blitz, so the maximum time a game can take is ten minutes. This way, a round-robin tournament with fifteen to twenty players can finish in one night.)

Some clubs have chess libraries available to members, some provide access to chess lessons or lectures by the club pro or a visiting master. Some sponsor simultaneous exhibitions or tournaments. The variety and amount of service to members provided by any particular club is only subject to the dedication and energy of the people who run it.

The Decline of Clubs

Late in the twentieth century the Swiss tournament took hold of the imagination of American chess players. A typical tournament usually took up an entire weekend and often involved some serious travel expenses.

Many players addicted to playing chess couldn't keep up all their club activities and play the tournament circuit. So these players would frequent weekend tournaments more and more, and their local club less and less.

FACT

A pervasive part of modern society, the Internet brings like-minded people together and estranges them at the same time. Anyone with Internet access can now play a game of chess with a faceless opponent from anywhere on earth at any given hour, day or night. Thus both opponents got a game and communicated, but there was no face-to-face human interaction.

This trend has continued with the advent of Internet chess play, where the club comes to the player rather than the other way around.

Chess Instruction

Many people want to improve their results or learn more about the game. This can be accomplished in any number of ways, including:

- Reading instructional material.
- Playing strong opponents.
- Analyzing your own games.
- Attending lectures.
- Finding a chess teacher.
- Developing a plan that includes all of the above.

How far you take such instruction is entirely up to you. This book may be enough to allow you to enjoy chess as a hobby for the rest of your life. Or you may want to improve enough to have a real chance to defeat a particular opponent or reach a particular rating. If you do decide to get serious about chess and wish to become a strong player or a champion, you will need to delve into many years of striving to master the game.

ALERT!

A good plan for improving your chess play will include all the listed elements. Whether you do this face to face or via correspondence or use books and magazines or videos or the Internet or software is irrelevant. How much material you retain and use is much more to the point.

Strong Chess

Playing a strong game means understanding what is required in many different types of positions. Many players divide these types of positions into the various opening systems, endgames where there are very few pieces on the board, and middlegame structures where different strategies need to be mastered.

Others aim for types of positions that suit their personality. Do you like to attack? Then learn which positions will give you the chance to launch a successful attack. Do you prefer defense? Then learn how to set up a successful defensive structure and how to beat back the attacks your opponents will throw at you. Just remember that good defenders are rare. Or maybe you prefer to counterattack or prevent strong attacks altogether.

Whatever types of positions or style of play you prefer, you will have to find a way to learn to understand what the pieces and pawns should be doing in many different positions. That may involve memorizing many different opening variations, combination themes, and endgame positions. And you could get them all wrong. That's why a good chess teacher is probably the most important learning tool you can invest in.

Fun with Chess

Most people who play chess do so for fun, without any aspirations of mastering the game. For you, none of the above is too relevant. Find what competition you can handle, and play. Or follow whatever chess news and/or games that interest you. If that's enough, you have a whole world of chess waiting for you.

Simultaneous Exhibitions

Picture a number of tables arranged in a rectangle or semicircle. There are chessboards on all the tables and people sitting in chairs along the outside at each board. They are all playing chess. But where is their opponent?

He or she is walking along the inner side of the tables, going from board to board, making moves. This is the chess master, and he or she is playing everybody else at the same time.

It's quite a spectacle. Usually the master will win many if not most of the games, and will lose very few, if any. Sometimes the master does this with a blindfold on. The players call out their moves to the master, and he/she calls out the response.

The number of opponents one master can handle in this way depends on the space available and the amount of players he or she can attract. Anywhere from two or three to hundreds of boards have been accommodated. More usual is between ten and fifty.

Numbers

Statistics are sometimes kept on simultaneous exhibitions, particularly if the master plays blind. World records have even been claimed for simultaneous games. But such exhibitions take a lot of time to complete, and some opponents leave before their games have gone very far. Those unfinished games are scored as another number for the master, and are usually claimed as a win as well.

FACT

Karl Podzielny played 575 games simultaneously in 1978. In 30½ hours he won 533, drew 27, and lost 15. Vlastimil Hort played 550 opponents, 201 simultaneously, and lost only 10 games in 1977. The late George Koltanowski played 56 consecutive (not simultaneous) blindfold games and won 50, drew 6 in San Francisco in 1960.

Tandem Simuls

Sometimes more than one master may be in the middle of a simultaneous exhibition. In such a case (a "tandem simul"), each one only plays every second or third move. This can provide a nice chance for the amateur opponents, since the masters may have different styles and thus trip each other up.

Another type of tandem simul is when there are multiple simultaneous exhibitions going on at the same time. This is a common occurrence in chess camps, and happens each year on the East Coast with the famous annual "Chessathon," where scores of masters volunteer to play hundreds of schoolchildren.

Composed Problems

A segment of the chess world has nothing to do with playing games. These are the people interested in composing or solving chess studies or problems.

Instead of beginning with the starting position, where the object of the game is to checkmate the opponent's king or at least prevent your own king from getting checkmated, such studies begin with whatever pieces and pawns the composer wants. There is a stipulation accompanying such studies such as White to play and checkmate Black in two moves (or six moves or any number of moves).

The appeal of such exercises is an aesthetic one. Solvers are testing themselves against the position, not against an opponent. And composers are trying to express something beautiful in the way the pieces cooperate with each other.

Here is an example of a mate in two:

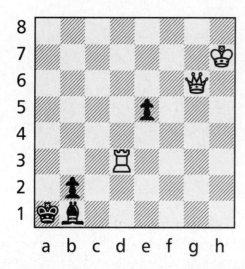

◀ White to move and mate in two moves.

This composition features the pin and the unpin. It is composed by V. Chepizhny and won first prize in the Nikolaev-200 competition in 1989. It appeared in the May 2000 *Chess Life*, submitted by columnist Robert Lincoln. Solution: **1. Qg1.**

And not 1. Rd1, when 1. ... Ka2 escapes the pin and the mate, though 1. ... e4, with an unpin, succumbs to 2. Qa6 mate.

1. ... Ka2 2. Qa7 mate or 1. ... e4 (with an unpin) 2. Ra3 mate.

The chess problem world has specialized terms, such as *self block*, *interference*, *battery* (two pieces or more on the same line, with at least one of them a long-range piece), and *excelsior* (a pawn starts out on its original square and takes either five or six moves to promote. The promotion, whether to a queen or an under-promotion, will produce checkmate).

Endgame Studies

These are a bit different than composed problems, in that there is no forced checkmate in so many moves. Also, there are usually fewer pieces on the board. The stipulation is usually White to move and win or draw.

Here is an example of an endgame study:

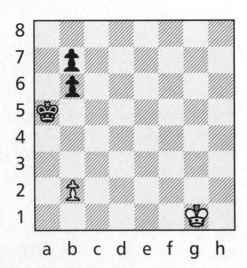

◀ White to play and draw.

This one was composed by Grigoriev in 1935 and appeared in Pal Benko's column in the April 2002 *Chess Life*.

Solution: **1. Kf2 Ka4 2. Ke3 b5 3. Ke4!! Kb4 4. Kd4 Kb3 5. Kd5! b4 6. Kc5 b6+ 7. Kb5** and the position is drawn.

Other moves by White lead to the same position. For instance, 2. ... Kb3 3. Kd4 or 2. ... Kb4 3. Kd3.

Helpmates

These compositions are completely strange to any chess competitor. Both sides, White and Black, cooperate in checkmating Black. And Black moves first.

Here is an example:

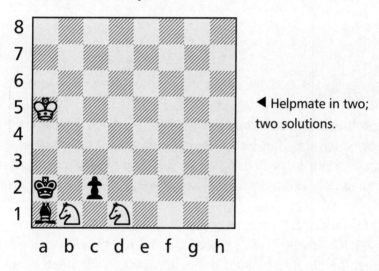

◀ Helpmate in two; two solutions.

This one was composed by J. Boggio and appeared in *Europe-Échecs* in 1962 and in *Chess Life* in September 2002.

In the solutions you will note that Black's move is given first. It looks strange for a Black move to be recorded first, but Helpmates are strange to begin with.

Solution 1: 1. cxb1=R Ka4 2. Rb2 Nc3 mate.
Solution 2: 1. cxd1=N Kb4 2. Nb2 Nc3 mate.

The themes of underpromotion, self-block, and interference predominate.

Serious Competition

If casual play or simuls or problems are not to your liking, or if they are not enough, there's always serious competition to be had, either in some rated tournament or match.

Structured competition in the United States outside the club became quite big in the latter half of the twentieth century. This came with the introduction of the Swiss-system tournament, which allows every competitor to play five or six games in a weekend. In a Swiss-system tournament, you play somebody with the same or a similar score throughout the event.

Matches

This was always and still is the essence of chess. You and me: Let's find out who plays better chess.

A match between two strong players that is rated and sanctioned and followed by fans can be exhilarating. But you don't have to be a champion or even a very strong player to get a similar exhilaration. All you need is a willing opponent somewhere close to your own strength.

If you want an audience, set up your match for a mall or an outdoor festival. If you'd rather just slug it out in private, somebody's home or at the library are good enough. All you really need is an appropriate opponent who is willing to engage you in the match.

For any scheduled chess game, it is important to show up on time. Failure to do so is not only rude; it also could damage your chances in the game. In a timed encounter, your clock is set ticking when the game is scheduled. If you fail to show up in the next hour, you forfeit the game.

Tournaments

Formal tournaments come in various types, and most people are familiar with at least several of those types. Tournaments are held in many sports and games, including scrabble, bridge, and tennis.

The types of tournaments used for chess tournaments include:

1. Round-robin
2. Double round-robin
3. Knockout
4. Swiss system

The round-robin is a very basic device that can handle a few people in a short time or a lot of people over a long period of time. Every competitor plays every other competitor. If there are eight players, each one will play seven games.

Another version of the round-robin is the double round-robin. Each player gets a game with White and a game with Black with every other competitor. This way, nobody has any inherent advantage. The obvious disadvantage is that playing two games against each of your seven opponents means playing fourteen games. And that may take a long time.

The round-robin and especially the double round-robin has been the staple of professional chess for a long time. But such tournaments typically take a few weeks to a month to complete, especially when professionals insist on playing only one game a day.

Most people simply don't have the time or the resources or the energy to go through such a brutal schedule. So the alternate systems are much more appropriate for the casual player or even the serious amateur.

If you are familiar with the knockout system, this probably comes from watching tennis. You play until you lose. At the end, only one player remains as the champion. This is an exciting type of tournament, but hasn't really caught on in the chess community.

The tournament of choice for most chess players in the United States is the Swiss system, which is essentially a knockout format with nobody getting eliminated. When you lose, you simply play someone else who has lost. But it resembles a knockout for the winners.

Ranking

Ranking is important for a Swiss-system tournament. For that, chess players use their ratings. The competitors are divided into two groups for the first round. The top player in the top group plays the top player in the bottom group, the second player in the first group plays the second player in the bottom group, etc. In subsequent rounds, the players are divided up by score group. In the third round, all those with three wins are in one group, those with two and a half comprise the next score group, those with two another, etc. Each score group is divided in two, with the top player from the top group playing the top player from the bottom group.

Correspondence Chess

Playing chess through the mail is not an activity for impatient people. A game can take over a year to complete, with moves coming on a weekly basis rather than within seconds (also known as *blitz chess*) or minutes.

Correspondence in general is mostly a faded memory of what it used to be, and correspondence chess is no exception. Our modern world includes TV, radio, telephone, e-mail, faxes, and the Internet. These have all eroded our need for correspondence, but have also provided us with alternate ways to communicate. Thus there are telephone, e-mail, and Internet chess competitions as well as the more traditional face-to-face and correspondence games.

FACT

There are sanctioned correspondence tournaments where you pay a fee and can earn a prize. These events are rated, just like over-the-board (OTB) tournaments. There are arbiters, or referees, to make sure the event runs smoothly and everyone sends their moves in on time.

Of course chess notation is what makes correspondence chess possible. You simply write your move on a letter or postcard and send it off. It's a good idea to include the last couple of moves, and even a diagram if you can. And it's also a good idea to keep a separate board handy that has the current position on it. This is true especially if you have more than one game going.

Chess Books and Magazines

A huge number of chess books and magazines are available to the enthusiast. It has been claimed that there are more books on chess than on all other books combined. And more are being written every day. The USCF has a large collection of chess books and magazines available through the Web site ✍ *www.uschess.org*, the USCF catalog, or the sales hotline ✆ 1-800-388-KING (5464).

Subject Matter

These books cover a bewildering array of chess material. The subject matter of these works can range from spot the checkmate and find the combination themes to pamphlets and even large tomes devoted to a subvariation of one of the openings. It can include explanations of how to handle isolated pawn positions or collections of some of the great games. There are books devoted to endgame studies or historical changes in style. Somewhere along the way, every conceivable area of the game is covered.

FACT

The most popular chess books in the United States are those on the openings. Whether the multivolume reference works that cover all the main openings or the specialty books that cover the latest trends in certain variations or the how-to instructions on specific openings or variations, these opening books are in great demand.

Magazines

Besides the official national chess magazine, *Chess Life*, there are official state magazines for practically every state, correspondence chess magazines, problem magazines, even a blitz chess magazine! With resources like that, you will never run out of reading material. This doesn't include the various club bulletins and local publications that come and go. And we haven't even touched on the Internet yet.

Chess in Education

There is a concerted effort these days to get chess into primary and secondary schools, either as an after-school activity or as a required subject. Some school administrators and teachers have become convinced that the act of learning chess increases cognitive skills and self-esteem.

There have been several studies done, using scientific criteria, to determine what learning chess can do for students. If these studies are accurate, the unmistakable conclusion is that when students learn chess, they learn to make decisions, plan ahead, accept the consequences of their decisions, think analytically, and thus improve self-esteem.

Another reason chess in the schools is such a good idea is the great amount of transferability involved. Skills learned through chess can transfer to skills in math, geography, English, foreign languages, science, finance, art, and many other subjects.

These studies have taken place using grade school students as the subjects, and they have taken place among privileged subjects as well as at-risk subjects. The results are always the same. Whether rich or poor, whether taken from good families or socially and/or financially challenged families, students who learn chess seem to improve their thinking skills.

Other Forms of Chess

There are other games that use most of the rules of chess and the same equipment. Some of these are popular, and some have been almost forgotten. Others are being invented as you read.

Bughouse

Very popular with the younger crowd, this version of chess requires two boards, two sets, and four players. It is real team chess, with each team consisting of two players. One plays White on one board, while the other plays Black on the other board. When a piece or pawn is captured, it does not simply leave the board. It becomes the property of your teammate. When you have acquired extra pieces or pawns in this way, you can use one of them by placing it anywhere on the board (with certain restrictions) in place of making a normal move.

ALERT!

There are thousands of chess variants, ranging from three-dimensional chess to versions that add squares to the board and pieces to the set. Older versions also exist, such as Chinese and Japanese chess, which are closer to the original Indian or Persian game. But none of them has gathered the great popularity of the royal game that we all know.

Fischer Random

This is chess with a different starting position. A computer will generate your starting position, which can be almost anything as long as the pieces begin on the first and eighth ranks and the pawns begin on the seventh and second ranks. Certain restrictions apply to castling and the bishops must be on opposite colors.

Another, similar, idea is called *prechess*. The game begins with only the pawns on the board, and each player's first eight moves consist of placing his pieces somewhere on the first rank (for White) or the eighth rank (for Black). Again, the bishops must occupy opposite color squares.

The reason for these variations is simply that openings have been studied so intensely for the last couple hundred years that many players feel this tremendous body of knowledge takes away any possible creativity in the openings.

Giveaway

In this version, the object of the game is not checkmate. Rather, the object is to give away every piece and pawn. Besides being able to ignore check and checkmate with impunity, the other peculiarity of giveaway is that captures are mandatory. E

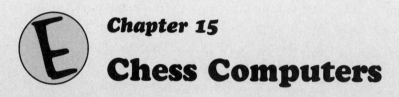

Chapter 15

Chess Computers

Twenty or more years ago, when IBM produced the first computers, did we ever think that one day we'd be playing chess on a computer? Probably not. But technology, being what it is, has found a way to give us what we like and what we want right in the palm of our hands.

A Modern Invention

Considering that chess started around A.D. 600, and computers only came on the scene a mere two to three decades ago, it would seem that chess and computers wouldn't mix. But the modern invention of computers that can play against people, play itself, analyze games, and run software that can teach you chess is an amazing modern invention. But, using artificial intelligence (AI), can computers really a match a person's ability to think through complicated moves to the finish? Realistically, computers are only as smart as they are programmed to be.

David Levy's Challenge

Back in 1970, when computers were first starting to play chess, International Master David Levy issued a £10,000 challenge to any programmer, stating that no computer could defeat him in a match within ten years. He later collected on his bet, defeating the best program of the day. He renewed the bet, and again collected, this time in 1990 versus Hans Berliner's Deep Thought. But by then the computers were starting to offer real resistance, and he did not renew the challenge the third time.

Kasparov Versus Deep Blue

By the early 1990s, chess-playing computers had reached grandmaster level. There weren't many players left who could defeat them when they were allowed to play at their best. They had been banned from tournament chess for some time.

Finally, the world champion of the time, Garry Kasparov, consented to play a highly publicized match with IBM's Deep Blue. He defeated the machine in 1996, 4 to 2, but the match was close, and he did lose one game.

ALERT!

In October 2002, humanity got a measure of revenge when BrainGames World Chess Champion Vladimir Kramnik played an eight-game match with Deep Fritz, one of the strongest computers available. The match ended in a tie, with Kramnik winning two early games and Fritz rallying to win two late games. The other four games were drawn.

Deeper Blue defeated Garry Kasparov in 1997. Surprisingly, it was not the tremendous look-ahead capability of the machine (it analyzed 200 million moves per second) that allowed it to triumph. Rather, it was Kasparov's surprise at its positional sophistication and his subsequent emotional collapse that allowed the machine to win. Kasparov resigned game two in a drawn position and made an uncharacteristic error in game six, and these were the two games he lost.

FACT

The human-computer match played in New York City between Kasparov and Deep Junior ended in a draw in February 2003. Each competitor won one game and drew the other four.

Machines That Play Chess

Everything from a mainframe, such as IBM's Deep Blue, to the smallest handheld devices can be programmed to play chess. If you want to go beyond the world of Internet chess, and take your chess game with you everywhere you go, you can now do so with the advent of the Palm Pilot machines, and other portable types of handheld devices that feature chess games. Are you traveling, or do you like to sit in front of the television and play games? With the handheld computer device called a PDA—personal digital assistant—you can keep your address book and date book up-to-date while you play your games.

ESSENTIAL

Some chess-playing computers make their own moves. Instead of having to punch in the notation for your move and reading and interpreting the computer's answer, you simply make your move and wait for a reply. The computer will make its own move. This is done by using interior magnets.

Some computers are programmed to talk to you. They may offer advice to help you play better or snide comments, depending on the humor of the programmer. Such programs show a clear intent to replace your usual human opponent. As such, they will never succeed. But isn't it amazing what these machines can do?

Software That Plays Chess

There are many, many software programs that can be loaded into your computer, your handheld, or these days, your cell phone that will allow you to play chess against a machine. Most software is Windows-based, but there is plenty out there for Macintosh and DOS enthusiasts. The USCF has a large collection of chess software available through the Web site ✐*www.uschess.org*, the USCF catalog, or the sales hotline ✆1-800-388-KING (5464).

Chessmaster

At this writing, Chessmaster has just released the 9000 version of chess software program. This is probably one of the best products in terms of features (what it offers) and benefits (what it does) and price. Load Chessmaster onto your computer and you can begin to play immediately. You can even play interactively with someone else via the Internet or e-mail. It also features online help, a training module, and analysis.

Computer software that plays chess can be an exceptionally good training tool. Or it can be just plain fun (or just plain frustrating, depending on the level you set the software to play at). Most available packages have something of everything: a database of games, the ability to play you or itself, the ability to analyze each move and give the results of its analysis. You can probably learn more sitting at your computer for a couple hours than you ever could simply reading a chess book. It's that interactive part that is such a wonderful coaching device.

Focus

Other software modules include programs that focus specifically on tutorials, or on games played by grandmasters with their notes so you can study their moves. And others offer specific opening, middlegame, and endgame sequences, as well as specific strategies and tactics such as the Dragon and Najdorf variations of the Sicilian Defense. Many computer software programs have an extensive library of games, and allow you to download other, newer games to your computer.

Analysis Engines

If you want to analyze your games, or the games of another, analysis engines rank at the top in allowing you to separate out every move and decide whether or not it was a good move or a weak move. In addition, analysis engines will even suggest other moves that you might have made instead.

But you must beware. Computers still have a different way of "looking at" positions than humans do. Psychological considerations don't come into their thoughts at all, and humans often need this element in order to play well.

ALERT!

When purchasing a chess-playing software package or an analysis engine, make sure it is compatible with your computer. All software comes with an indication of system requirements. Make sure you know that these are minimum requirements. It is usually better to have more capabilities than you need.

Also, the computers are not perfect yet. They still evaluate positions where one side has a lot of material as a win for that side unless there is a forced sequence of moves ending in checkmate for the side with the lesser material. And sometimes that sequence of moves is there, but it is too far off in the future for the analysis engine to pick up on it.

Chess Databases

Just like a regular database that provides sorting capabilities, so too a chess database provides a lot of material that is sortable. With this database you can sort information on chess players, their games, and more. If you would like to know about all the games played by a particular grandmaster in a specific period of time, using a specific opening, a chess database will provide that information for you. You can zero in on your special interest and save your sorted information for review over and over.

Serious chess players use these powerful chess databases to keep track of different games so they can drill themselves. Casual chess players and serious chess players alike can enter their own games into these databases and keep track of them.

CDs

Most computer programs these days come resident on a CD that you insert into your computer from which you upload the information. CDs are a big advantage over floppy disks that hold only a certain amount of information. CDs allow the programmer to provide you with all of the source code (which you generally cannot get at) that's required to operate the software. You must of course, have a computer that accepts CDs and that has enough memory on your hard drive to accept the program, and enough RAM (random access memory) to allow the program to work well.

You can also download, for a fee, software directly from the manufacturer or programmer through the Internet. Some companies will allow you to download a modified version of their software as a demo so you can test it out before you plunk down your hard-earned money. This is an effective way of deciding which program is really right for you. Usually you can test the software for thirty days before it "disappears" or is no longer available for your use.

Handheld computers like the Palm Pilot allow you, with enough resident memory, to play chess in the palm of your hand. You will play chess against the device (the computer) or against another person, using the PDA as your chess set. As an alternative, you can purchase any number and types of chess games that can be loaded onto your desktop computer.

ChessBase

Perhaps the top chess database is ChessBase, which also offers a version for the Macintosh. But ChessBase has something else. It comes with analysis engines, such as Fritz, Junior, and Hiarcs. These are some of the top analysis engines available. There is also *ChessBase* magazine, which is available either from the Internet or via CD. This magazine allows users to be aware of the latest upgrades of the software package, the latest additions of other software, and the latest games being played around the world.

Upgrading capability via CD or the Internet is becoming common in software of all types. Chess players of today thus have a big advantage over their counterparts of yesterday in the tremendous availability of material on the game—that is, if you have the time and money needed to peruse it all.

Online Chess

The Internet has opened up a whole new world of gaming. And if you want to play chess with someone, but can't or won't do it by playing in a face-to-face tournament, or you aren't a fan of correspondence chess, then the Internet offers so many possibilities for engaging in your pastime.

It's becoming increasingly popular for people to play chess online—many sites spring up each day. There are numerous Web-based sites for different types of OTB (over-the-board) play. If you are at work, or at home working on your computer and you need a short diversion, a quick computer chess game can be just the thing for you.

If you play online chess, it's considered bad form, and is also against the official rules and regulations, to use a computer to help you win. A game is supposed to be between two players, not two players with helpers. Policing this rule is a real challenge for Internet and correspondence tournament directors, as you might expect.

How Can I Play Online?

Internet chess play is an interactive way of playing OTB chess without having to leave the comfort of your home or office. As long as you have a connection to the Internet, you can play chess. That means that you can play in a car, on a plane, through your laptop, or at your desktop computer.

Different sites offer different things, but generally all sites offer interactive play, ratings, discussions groups, information on chess software, chess databases, and a place for further reading and study. In addition, you can usually get a rating after each game played, and many sites offer lectures with grandmasters and other top players. Visiting several sites to get a feel for the atmosphere and how chess is played will give you an idea of what the various sites have to offer.

Internet Chess Clubs

Chess games can be played in real time, similar to playing games of chess via telephone. Clubs also offer information and discussion about databases, games collections, chess-playing software, and other computer programs of a similar nature, either offered for sale, or in the state of development.

As you start to log on to the various chess servers, you'll undoubtedly come across something called PGN, which stands for Portable Game Notation. This is a special computer format used for encoding chess games so they can be easily sorted and retrieved. PGN notation can be opened in your favorite (major) word processor, which will show notations as text, or you can download a software program that recognizes PGN and will display it on your computer.

If you don't know where to look for a chess game, start with one of the search engines such as Google, Alta Vista, Yahoo!, or Lycos. Type "chess games" in the search field, and watch what happens. You'll be presented with a myriad of sites that will allow you to play chess. Some charge a fee, some are for members only, and some may be free. But generally you can find a game twenty-four hours of the day, seven days a week.

Many sites allow you to play games using any time control you and your opponent agree to, ranging from one minute for the whole game to five or more hours. You can also get ratings, blitz, and slow chess. Each game is rated immediately after it is played, but if you prefer, you can play unrated games too.

A unique feature is that you can watch a variety of other players, use special graphical interfaces that allow you to make your moves using a mouse on your screen (the old drag and drop technique), talk to anyone from around the world, or even participate or watch simultaneous matches.

U.S. Chess Live

The USCF has its own chess Web site where you can connect to its online chess service, called U.S. Chess Live. Start at ✍ *www.uschess.org* and then click on the USCL banner. U.S. Chess Live is a service that allows you to connect with others who want to play chess online. You can also shop for products and equipment, catch up on lectures and the latest moves, participate in events, and, if you have a problem or a chess-related question, you can pose it to the administrator. You can also volunteer your time to work with other players, or participate as a lecturer in the Scout Chess program for Girl Scouts and Boy Scouts. The USCL online playing site features:

- A built-in database to save and analyze all of your games.
- Direct point-and-click access to join tournaments, lectures, and other events.
- A redesigned game board featuring attractive time clocks, time of move and lag time display, and figurine notation.
- An integrated profile system that organizes member profiles and player information, such as ratings and saved games, into easily accessed folders.

- A message system with a traditional e-mail interface to keep in touch with your chess friends.
- Lecture-on-demand capabilities.

Royal Membership

USCL offers a Royal Membership service that gives access to weekly events including Battle of the Minds, Master Challenges, Chess Simuls, and Guess the Moves contests for prizes. In addition, Royal Members receive access to the exclusive Chess University, featuring top chess professionals and passage to a large database of interactive chess lectures. Free entry to a vast library of past lectures that are playable on demand at your convenience is also available.

Internet Sources

Besides the U.S. Chess Live site and the ChessBase site mentioned previously, there are an unbelievable amount of chess sites out there in cyberspace.

Online Magazines and News Groups

If you like to read your information online, there's plenty of chess available. The list is so vast that it's impossible to list them all. Suffice it to say that each of the major chess servers has its own version of online chess news to keep you up-to-date. And if you are playing chess online, you should be able to access news and information through these sources.

Some of the major sources include:

- USCF (*www.uschess.org*)
- New In Chess (*www.newinchess.com*)
- *Chess Monthly* Magazine (*www.chess.co.uk*)
- This Week in Chess (*www.chesscenter.com/twic/twic.html*)
- Europe Échecs (*www.europe-echecs.com*)
- World Chess Hall of Fame and Sidney Samole Museum (*www.worldchesshalloffame.com*)

- ChessBase (✐ *www.chessbase.com*)
- ChessCafe (✐ *www.chesscafe.com*)

Each online server should have a step-by-step guide on how to start your own computer account, how to manage and maintain it, and what policies to adhere to. You can also download most popular chess engines and learn about other computers playing online.

If you are looking to play casual chess online, it's best to go to one of the general game sites. However, if you are looking for hard-core chess, you'll want to check out specific chess gaming sites such as USCL (U.S. Chess Live) or the ICC (Internet Chess Club). They run tournaments and many other feature events, and are populated with many strong and famous players.

Additionally, you should be able to find and play in tournaments, view others' games, visit with top-rated players on special events and online talks, and view your standings. Most online servers also have chess experts who are willing to devote their time and effort to help beginning chess players to improve their game.

Some Features

Diagrams, commentary on games, news, politics, and more are included on many sites. In addition, you can also see live coverage of many scholastic and national and international championships. In many cases you can see the games as they are being played and you may also be able to hear a grandmaster commentary on the play-by-play. Also, each week interesting articles, interviews, chess problems, and all of the games of significant tournaments are published and posted to various sites.

Internet chess clubs are also a great way to get information about chess books and equipment. If you can't decide which book to purchase or which computer chess game is better for your kid, then you can read more about the product online, or you can ask the experts.

Types of Events

Many people are familiar with the famous game played by Garry Kasparov against the world. This was an online chess game held in 1999. Microsoft sponsored the event, Kasparov had White, and his opponent (the world) had Black. Anyone could go to the Web site and register a single vote for a chess move. Whichever move won the vote would be played against Kasparov. Each side had one day to play a move.

Kasparov had a rough time with this game. There were several professional chess players who offered their advice to the world, so the move that won turned out to be quite good. Kasparov was surprised out of the opening and so the game became a real fight. In fact, the world could have drawn an endgame, but there was disagreement over which move to play, and the wrong move won. Ⓔ

Glossary

adjust: A player, when it is his turn to move, may adjust (slide a chessman to the center of the square) pieces by first announcing "*j'adoube*" or "I adjust."

attack: Various ways to try breaking down your opponent's defense.

back rank mate: This is a mate that occurs on any row (rank or file) at the edge of the board.

battery: Any two long-range pieces of the same color lined up along one line of attack.

Black: The dark pieces are referred to as Black in chess, regardless of their actual color.

blindfolded chess: A game of chess that is played by one or both opponents without the sight of a board and pieces.

bishop: A piece that moves on diagonals, any number of squares, and starts out next to the king and queen. Each player gets two: one that travels on light-square diagonals, and one that travels on dark-square diagonals.

capture: A pawn or piece may be captured (taken) when an opponent's piece may legally move to the square the pawn or piece occupies.

castling: A player moves the king two squares to the right or left toward one of his rooks. The rook is then moved to the opposite side of the king and placed on the adjacent square. Neither piece may have moved before, and the king may not castle into, out of, or through check.

center: It is important to fight for control of the center of the board. Central development allows for greater mobility and space for the pieces.

check: A move that places the king under attack is a *check*.

checkmate: When the king is under attack and there is no legal way to get the king out of check, it is called *checkmate*.

chessboard: A checkered board with sixty-four squares in an eight-by-eight arrangement.

chess clock: A device with two clocks connected to keep track of each individual's time during a chess game.

chess computer: A computer dedicated solely to playing chess.

chess etiquette: The rules of conduct that govern chess play. These rules of conduct are good manners, but also laws of chess.

combination: A series of moves combining tactical weapons to gain an advantage.

convergence: Any two or more pieces or pawns of the same color lined up to threaten an enemy square, piece, or pawn.

coordinate squares: An endgame situation in which certain squares are linked to other squares. When the enemy king goes to one square, your king must be able to get to its corresponding square.

defense: Various ways to hold back or neutralize your opponent's threats.

desperado: A tactic in which a piece or pawn that is lost in any case captures an enemy piece or pawn to take along with it.

development: Moving the pieces from their starting squares, usually toward the center of the board. This is the major goal of the opening.

discovered attack: A surprise attack created when one piece moves and uncovers an attack by another piece on the same rank, file, or diagonal.

discovered check: A type of discovered attack that places the king in check.

double attack: A situation in which two or more enemy squares, pieces, and/or pawns are threatened simultaneously.

double check: A discovered check that attacks the king with two pieces.

draw: A tie game. No one wins.

endgame: The portion of the game in which so many pieces have been captured that the kings can take an active part in the battle.

en passant: This is a French term that means "in passing." When one player moves a pawn two squares to try to escape capture by the opponent's pawn, the pawn is captured *in passing* as though it had only moved one square.

en prise: A French term meaning "in take." A piece is en prise when it is under attack and undefended.

Exchange: A term for the trading of a rook for a minor piece, e.g., winning a rook for a bishop or a knight is called *winning the Exchange*.

fianchetto: The development of the bishop to b2, g2, b7, or g7.

file: A vertical row of squares running between the two opponents. These rows are named by letters: a, b, c, d, e, f, g, and h.

forced move: A move that would lead to a lost position, if not made.

fork: All pieces and pawns are capable of forking. This special tactic by a single piece or pawn occurs when it attacks two or more of the opponent's pieces.

half-open file: A file that has a pawn of only one color on it is half open; the side without a pawn has a half-open file.

happy pieces and pawns: Any piece or pawn that is at full strength, making use of its potential.

j'adoube: French for "I adjust." A player, when it is his turn to move, may adjust (slide a chessman to the center of the square) pieces by first announcing "*j'adoube*" or "I adjust."

king: The most important piece in a chess game. When the king is trapped (this is called *checkmate*), the game is over, with the side that trapped his opponent's king victorious. This monarch moves one square at a time in any direction, and has the option once a game to castle.

king safety: Since he is the whole game, it makes sense to keep your king safe behind a wall of pawns until the danger of checkmate is much reduced.

kingside: The half of the board from the e-file to the h-file.

knight: Shaped like a horse's head, this chess piece

leaps over all adjacent squares to a different colored square. Each player gets two, and they begin the game between the bishops and the rooks.

long-range pieces: Queens, rooks, and bishops. These are pieces that can cover an entire open line in one move.

looking ahead: Visualizing a new position after one or more potential moves without actually disturbing the position.

major pieces: The rooks and queen; the pieces that have the potential for controlling the most squares.

mate: Short for checkmate.

mini-battery: A battery consisting of a queen or bishop as the base and a pawn as the front, lined up along the diagonal where the pawn can capture.

minor pieces: The bishops and knights; these pieces generally control fewer squares than the queen and rook.

no retreat: A situation in which a piece has nowhere safe to go.

notation: A system for recording the moves of a chess game.

open file: A file that has no pawns on it.

opening: The part of the game that is used to develop the pieces.

opposition: A technique used to force the opponent's king to move away by placing your king typically with one square between them on a rank or file.

pieces: Kings, queens, rooks, bishops, and knights are the pieces in chess.

pawns: The little guys that line up in front of the pieces at the start of a game. They have a distinctive type of move with many exceptions. Pawns have always been the foot soldiers of chess, and each player starts out with eight.

passed pawn: A pawn that has no enemy pawns in front of it on the same file or on either adjacent file.

pawn promotion: When a piece reaches the final row on the opposite side of the board, it has the option of becoming a queen, rook, bishop, or knight.

pin: A tactic that "sticks" or "pins down" one piece to another along a rank, file, or diagonal. If the piece is pinned to the king, it is illegal to move the pinned piece, for it would expose the king to check.

queen: Each player gets only one. She can move in any straight line, along ranks, files, or diagonals, any number of squares.

queenside: The half of the chessboard from the d-file to the a-file.

rank: A row that runs from left to right across the board. The numbered rows on marked chessboards.

removing the defender: A tactic that removes the defender of a given square, piece, or pawn, so that it is no longer defended.

rook: The rook moves along ranks or files, any number of squares, and is capable of castling with the king occasionally. It starts out in the corners when a game begins, and each player gets two.

sacrifice: Giving up material to gain a greater advantage. Often used for attacking the king.

skewer: The skewer is a backward pin. It is an attack on two pieces on the same rank, file, or diagonal, but, unlike the pin, it forces the closer piece to move, which leaves the other piece to be captured.

sleeping pieces: Pieces that have nothing to do, such as the long-range pieces at the start of a game.

stalemate: A tie game that results from the opponent with more material controlling all the squares around the weaker side's king but not directly attacking the king.

strategy: Strategy deals with overall plans or goals as opposed to tactical calculations.

tactics: The "fireworks" of chess are "tricks" or weapons used to win material or gain some other advantage. They include convergence, batteries, pins, forks, skewers, discovered attacks, removing defenders, no retreat, desperado, Zwischenzug, and opposition.

threats: Any potential capture or promotion that will gain value, or any potential check, checkmate, stalemate, or other type of draw. All pieces and pawns are capable of making threats.

three-position repetition: A type of draw in which the same position, with the same player to move, is repeated for the third time during the course of a game.

touch move: In chess if you touch a piece without saying "I adjust" first, then you must move it.

tournament chess: An event where chess games are played against more than one opponent.

value of the pieces: The value of a piece depends on how many squares it attacks; therefore, the value will change depending upon where the piece is located on the board. Remember, however, your king is worth the game!

waking up the pieces: At the start of the game, all pieces are very sleepy (they have nothing to do). Waking them up means giving them lines and squares to go to so they can realize their potential strength.

White: The light pieces are referred to as White in chess, regardless of their actual color.

winning the Exchange: If you win a rook for a bishop or a knight, you have won the Exchange.

Zugzwang: A German word that means one is forced to move but has no good options.

Zwischenzug: A German word that refers to an in-between move.

Appendix B
Frequently Asked Questions

CONFUSED? Is your head spinning? Do you still have questions after reading this book? Are you afraid to ask? Well, here are the most frequently asked questions about chess. You'll find answers to your questions here.

Q **What is a rating?**

A rating is a number that generally ranges between 100 and 2,800. The average rating for scholastic players nationwide is about 700. Ratings are a measure of past tournament performance. Anyone who plays in a USCF-sanctioned tournament receives a national rating. When you win games your rating goes up, and when you lose games your rating goes down. The number of rating points that you gain (or lose) depends upon your rating and the rating of your opponent. Your rating appears on your *Chess Life* magazine label, the address label that allows the magazine to come to you. The USCF provides a national rating service that can be used to compare players from different parts of the country. Separate rating systems are maintained for over-the-board (OTB) chess, correspondence chess, online chess, and quick chess. These rating systems are totally independent from one another. Some chess organizations also maintain local or regional rating systems, and the World Chess Federation (FIDE) maintains an international rating system.

Q **What is the difference between a provisional and an established rating?**

A provisional rating is a rating that is based on four to twenty-five games. An established rating is based on twenty-six or more games. Note that a player who has played less than four rated games does not receive a rating. A player with a provisional rating is not unrated. Provisional ratings are used for tournament pairing purposes in exactly the same way that established ratings are used. However, a player with a provisional rating is not eligible to be included on the top 100 lists.

Q **What is chess notation or "scorekeeping"?**

Players can use chess notation to make a record of the moves that they make during a chess game. This is called *keeping score* of the game. The most popular system of chess notation is the algebraic system, but some players still use the older descriptive system. In most tournaments, players are required to keep score of their games. However, in quick chess tournaments and some scholastic tournaments, score keeping is optional.

Q **What is algebraic notation?**

Algebraic notation is the most popular form of chess notation. Each of the files (vertical columns) of a chessboard is labeled with a lowercase letter, and each of the ranks (horizontal rows) of a chessboard is labeled with a number. Starting on White's left side, the eight files are identified with the letters a to h. Starting at White's end of the board, each of the ranks is numbered 1 to 8. Each square is identified using the letter of its file and the number of its rank. Thus, the starting square for White's queen rook is a1, and the starting square for Black's king rook is h8. Pieces are identified using capital letters: K for king, Q for queen, R for rook, B for bishop, N for knight, and P (or no letter at all) for pawn. To write a chess move, write the uppercase letter for the piece that is moving followed by the name of the square that the piece is moving to. For example, if White begins by moving the pawn in front of his king two squares forward and Black responds by moving his king's knight toward the center of the board, these two moves would be written as 1. Pe4 Nf6 or 1. e4 Nf6. We encourage you to learn algebraic notation at the same time that you learn the rules of the game. It's much easier to talk about chess if you know the language.

Q How does someone become a chess master?
The USCF awards the National Master (NM) title to any player who earns an OTB rating of at least 2,200. A player who maintains an OTB rating of 2,200 over the course of 300 tournament games earns the title of Life Master, and a player who earns an OTB rating of 2,400 earns the title of Senior Master (SM). There are approximately 1,000 National Masters in the United States.

Q How does someone become a Grandmaster?
The Grandmaster (GM) title is awarded by the World Chess Federation (FIDE) to players who have achieved consistently strong results in international competition. There are approximately fifty GMs in the United States, and there are less than 1,000 GMs in the entire world.

Q What is FIDE?
FIDE (pronounced fee-day), the acronym for the World Chess Fédération, stands for Fédération Internationale des Échecs. FIDE is recognized by the International Olympic Committee as the governing body for international chess. FIDE organizes international chess championships, awards titles to successful players, and maintains ratings for the world's top chess players. The members of FIDE are national chess federations like the USCF.

Q What is U.S. Chess Live?
U.S. Chess Live is the USCF's official site for online chess, and it is available to all USCF members. To use the site, please visit ✍ *www.uschesslive.org* and download the free client software, and register. If you are not a USCF member, you will not be able to register. However, you will be able to log on to the site as a guest.

Q What kind of chess set and board should I buy?
We recommend solid plastic pieces using the standard Staunton design and a vinyl roll-up board with algebraic notation on the side. Hollow plastic pieces should be avoided since they break easily. Beginners should also avoid themed chess sets such as the *Star Wars* chess set or the *Simpsons* chess set since these pieces may be difficult to recognize.

Q Should I buy chess books for my child?
Chess books are a very inexpensive way for your child to acquire tremendous amounts of chess knowledge. If you have to force your child to read a chess book, then forget it. However, if your child wants to read chess books, then you should buy them. You should buy books for your child that contain lots of explanations in English (or whatever your native language might be) and avoid books that contain long lines of cryptic chess analysis without any explanation. *Pawn and Queen and in Between* by Frank Elley is a great starter book for young beginners. Your young chess player can then move on to the chess training materials by Chester Nuhmentz. Teenage beginners may prefer to start with *Comprehensive Chess Course*, volumes one and two by Lev Alburt. Your child might also enjoy *Bobby Fischer Teaches Chess* by Bobby Fischer, Stuart Margulies, and Donn Mosenfelder or *Winning Chess Strategy' for Kids* by Jeff Coakley. The USCF has a

large collection of chess books available through the Web site *www.uschess.org*, the USCF catalog, or the sales hotline ✆ 1-800-388-KING (5464).

Q Should I hire a chess teacher for my child?

Hiring a chess teacher is one of the most effective ways to learn chess. Unfortunately, it is also one of the most expensive ways to learn chess. The fees that chess teachers charge vary depending upon the teacher's knowledge, experience, and economic situation. Some nationally renowned chess teachers charge $80 per hour or more. If you know the rules of the game, you are fully qualified to be your child's first chess teacher. When your child starts to beat you regularly at chess, you might want to consider hiring a professional chess teacher.

Q Can the USCF recommend a good chess teacher?

The USCF usually does not recommend specific chess teachers. It is a national organization, and it often does not have information about the chess teachers in your local area. It recommends that you contact your state affiliate or your state scholastic coordinator. Links to state affiliate Web sites and state scholastic coordinators can be found at *www.uschess.org*.

Q What is a chess clock?

A chess clock is actually two separate clocks housed in a single casing. One clock keeps track of the time used by the player who is playing the White pieces, and the other clock keeps track of the time used by the player who is playing the Black pieces. There are two types of chess clocks, analog clocks and digital clocks. Digital clocks have a digital display for each player. When a player's digital display reaches zero, that player has run out of time. An analog clock has two traditional clock faces, one for each player. Each of these clock faces has a red flag. When a player is running low on time, the minute hand of the clock lifts the flag. When a player's flag falls, that player has run out of time. Analog clocks should be set so that a player's time expires when the clock reads six o'clock. A chess clock has two buttons, one for each player. When you are playing chess with a chess clock, make your move as usual and then use the same hand to press the nearer button on the clock. When you press the button, your clock will stop and your opponent's clock will start to run. If you run out of time and your opponent has enough material left on the board to checkmate you, your opponent can claim a win on time. If you run out of time and your opponent does not have enough material left on the board to checkmate you, your opponent can claim a draw. If your opponent does not notice that you have run out of time, you can continue to play the game and attempt to checkmate your opponent. If you checkmate your opponent before your opponent notices that you have run out of time, then you win the game.

Q Should I buy a chess clock for my child?

Serious tournament players need a chess clock, but beginners don't. Some serious tournament players will spend an hour on each move if given the opportunity, so chess clocks are needed at tournaments to ensure that all games end in a reasonable amount of time. However, most young beginners tend to make their moves too quickly and need to be encouraged to spend more time thinking about their moves. After your child has played in a couple of chess tournaments and expressed a desire to play in more tournaments, it's time to think about buying a chess clock. The USCF has a large collection of chess clocks available through the Web site *www.uschess.org*, the USCF catalog, or the sales hotline ✆ 1-800-388-KING (5464).

Q **Should I buy a chess computer?**

A chess computer is a wonderful tool. You don't need an expensive computer that is capable of challenging a chess master. Most computers have a variety of levels, and even the cheapest computers can challenge the average player. If you own a personal computer, you might prefer chess software instead of a stand-alone chess computer. Your child will probably prefer a kid-friendly product like Maurice Ashley Teaches Chess rather than a superstrong program like Fritz 6.0. Your child's silicon opponent will never get tired or bored with chess, so if your child wants to play chess more often than you do, it might be time to buy a chess computer or chess-playing software. The USCF has a large collection of chess computers available through the Web site ✐*www.uschess.org*, the USCF catalog, or the sales hotline ✆1-800-388-KING (5464).

Q **Should I buy a chess database?**

Databases are for serious chess players. Beginners learn very little from a chess database. When your child's rating has reached 1,600, you might want to buy ChessBase 8.0. Until then, don't worry about databases. The USCF has a large collection of chess databases available through the Web site ✐*www.uschess.org*, the USCF catalog, or the sales hotline ✆1-800-388-KING (5464).

Q **What is a chess camp?**

Theme camps are becoming very popular. There are baseball camps, soccer camps, and even chess camps. A chess camp is a summer camp where kids can go to learn about and play chess. Some chess camps are day camps, and other chess camps are sleep-over camps. Most chess camps offer some other activities such as swimming, soccer, tennis, etc. in addition to chess. For information about specific chess camps, please visit ✐*www.uschess.org*.

Q **What happens at a chess tournament?**

Chess players get together at chess tournaments to meet other chess players and enjoy several games of chess in a structured and sometimes competitive environment. Most chess tournaments are not elimination tournaments, so expect to play all of the scheduled rounds. Between scheduled tournament games, players eat, socialize, play casual (nontournament) chess games, or enjoy other activities. It is not uncommon for a game of soccer, tag, or basketball to spontaneously develop between the scheduled rounds of a scholastic chess tournament.

Q **When is my child ready to play in a chess tournament?**

Ask yourself two questions. Does my child know all the rules of the game? Does my child enjoy playing chess? If the answer to both of these questions is yes, then your child is probably ready to play in a chess tournament. Don't worry about how many games your child will win or lose. The goals for your child's first tournament should be to have fun playing chess and to make some new friends. Every child who enters his or her first tournament with these goals in mind will be a winner, no matter how many chess games are won or lost. You can find information about upcoming tournaments in the tournament life section of *Chess Life*.

Q **What should I bring to a chess tournament?**

You should bring your own chess set and board, since many chess tournament organizers do not provide boards and sets. You should bring a chess clock if you own one. We also recommended that your child have a pen or pencil and his or her own personal chess scorebook to keep a record of the games. At most large tournaments, there will be a concession area where you can purchase these supplies. It's a good idea to bring some snack food and a favorite quiet toy such as a coloring book or a handheld electronic game. A tournament is always more fun when your favorite food is available, and that toy may come in very handy during the downtime between tournament games.

Q What is the Swiss system?

The Swiss system is the most common system used for making pairings at chess tournaments. Swiss-system pairings match players against other players who have a similar or identical score. For example: in round two, players who won in round one are paired against other winners, and players who lost in round one are paired against other players who lost their first game. At the beginning of a tournament, there may be many mismatches. However, in the later rounds of a Swiss-system tournament, players often face opponents who are at approximately the same level of ability. One of the results of the Swiss system is that many players end the tournament with a roughly even score, such as 2 points out of four games.

Q What is a ½-point bye?

If you know that you will not be able to play in one of the scheduled rounds of a tournament, you may be allowed to take a ½-point bye. A player who has a ½-point bye receives a ½ point for the unplayed round. You will only receive a ½-point bye if you request it in advance. Some tournament organizers place restrictions on the number of ½-point byes that a player may take, and tournament advertising will often mention these restrictions.

Q What is a full-point bye?

If there are an odd number of players in a section of a tournament, then one of the players in that section will not have an opponent. If you are not able to play in a round of a tournament because you are the odd man out, you will receive a full-point bye. When it is necessary to award a full-point bye, the full-point bye is usually awarded to the lowest-rated player in the lowest score group who has not yet received a bye. The recipient of the full-point bye gets a full point without playing a game.

Q What is *blitz*?

Blitz chess is chess that is played very quickly. In a blitz game a chess clock is used and each player has a small amount of time (often five minutes) to complete the game. In order to win a blitz game, you must checkmate your opponent before you run out of time. Since there is not much time in a blitz game, blitz players must be thoroughly familiar with the rules of chess and have enough chess-playing experience to quickly make good chess decisions. The advantage to playing blitz is that many games can be played in a relatively short period of time.

Q What is *bughouse*?

Bughouse is a chess variant that is very popular with young players. Bughouse is a chess partnership. When playing bughouse, you play chess against an opponent, and your partner plays against your opponent's partner. When you capture a piece, you give it to your partner. When your partner captures a piece, he or she gives it to you. When it is your turn to move you may place a captured piece on the board instead of making a normal chess move. To find a complete set of bughouse rules, visit ✑ *www.kcrcc.org/supernationals*, click on "side events," click on "bughouse," and then follow the "rules" link.

Q What is *skittles*?

Skittles is the word that chess tournament players use for the casual games that they play before or after their serious tournament games. Many tournaments have a skittles area or a skittles room where players can go for skittles or analysis. It is very bad chess etiquette to play skittles games in the main playing hall of a tournament.

Q How much does USCF membership cost?

A one-year membership is currently $13 for scholastic members (age fourteen and under), $20 for youth members (age twenty-two and under), $30 for senior members (age sixty-five and over), $32 for Internet members, and $40 for regular adult members. (Please refer to ✍ *www.uschess.org* for updated rates.) Special rates are also available for blind members and prison members. Please note that Internet members do not receive a magazine. Discounted rates are also available for anyone who chooses to sign up for more than one year. (By the time you read this, membership rates may have changed. Please contact the membership department at the USCF at ✆ 1-800-388-5464 for current membership categories and prices.)

Q Should my child become a member of the USCF?

A USCF membership is a great value. If your child enjoys chess, the USCF and the authors encourage him or her to become a member.

Q What is a family membership?

Family membership is a special membership category available only if a member of your immediate family is a USCF member who lives with you and receives *Chess Life*. For example, if

your spouse is a regular USCF member, you may become a family member. For membership rates, please visit ✍ *www.uschess.org*. Family members do not receive a magazine but are entitled to all of the other benefits of USCF membership.

Q What are the benefits of USCF affiliation?

USCF affiliates receive a subscription to *Chess Life* and the USCF rating supplements, discounts on merchandise sold by the USCF, and a listing on the USCF Web site. USCF affiliates also have the right to run USCF-sanctioned tournaments and sell USCF memberships.

Q Should our chess club affiliate with the USCF?

We think so. We have more than 2,000 affiliates throughout the United States, and we hope that your club will join our happy family.

Q When is my child ready to play in a nation-al championship tournament?

Many of our national scholastic championships are open tournaments. You don't have to be a chess champion to participate. Thousands of players participate in our national scholastic championships each year. Many of these players are novices, and some are even playing in their first tournament. If your child knows all the rules of the game and enjoys playing chess, then your child is ready to play in a national championship tournament.

Q Why do chess tournaments have different sections?

Many large tournaments are divided into sections according to age, grade, or rating. This gives players an opportunity to play against opponents who are approximately the same age or ability level. For example, the National Scholastic K–12 Grade Chess Championship is divided into thirteen sections, one for each grade. At this tournament players must play in the section that corresponds to their grade. The National Elementary Chess Championship is divided into six sections, but players have more flexibility. At this tournament each section has an upper limit for a player's grade or rating. A third-grader with a rating below 800 could choose to play in the K-3 Under 800 section, the K-3 Championship section, the K-5 Under 1,000 section, the K-5 Championship section, the K-6 Under 1,000 section, or the K-6 Championship section, but a sixth-grader with a rating of 1,000 or higher is only eligible to play in the K-6 Championship section.

Q **Should my child play in "adult" tournaments?**

Most "adult" tournaments are actually open tournaments that are open to players of all ages. Some young players may be anxious about playing against adults, but open tournaments can be just as much fun as scholastic tournaments. Experienced chess coaches know that players who want to improve need to compete against challenging opponents. If your child is competing in scholastic tournaments and is winning more games than he or she is losing, it might be time to enter some "adult" tournaments in order to find some more challenging opponents.

Q **Can my child participate in international chess championships?**

Believe it or not, the answer to this question is "yes." Participation in some international championships, such as the World Youth Chess Championship, is limited to top-rated players. However, in recent years participation in the Pan-American Youth Championship has been open to all USCF members who are willing to pay their own expenses. Please contact *events@uschess.org* for more information.

Q **What is the Pressman All-America Chess Team?**

Every year the USCF recognizes the country's strongest young chess players. Players are selected according to their peak USCF rating. In order to be eligible for the Pressman All-America Team, a player must participate in at least four open, not scholastic, tournaments.

Q **What is *Chess Life*?**

Chess Life is a monthly magazine published by the USCF. It contains articles about chess, chess players, and chess tournaments, as well as a listing of upcoming chess tournaments throughout the United States. Most USCF members receive *Chess Life* as a benefit of being a USCF member. For membership rates, please visit *www.uschess.org*.

Q **How are the top 100 lists created?**

The top 100 lists are created once every two months in conjunction with the publication of the official rating supplements. They are published in the rating supplements and include only current USCF members with established ratings. Players whose membership is expired or who have provisional ratings are not included on these lists. Since the top 100 lists are updated only once every two months, the ratings that you see on the top 100 lists may not match the ratings that you see at the USCF Web site.

Q **What is the Chess for Youth Program?**

The Chess for Youth Program, sponsored by the U.S. Chess Trust, provides up to five free chessboards and sets and up to one free chess clock to schools that have chess programs. The U.S. Chess Trust also provides up to ten free USCF memberships to chess players who are on the federal free lunch program and who have never before been USCF members.

Q **What is the U.S. Chess Trust?**

The U.S. Chess Trust is a nonprofit organization that promotes the game of chess in the United States. The trust provides free chess equipment for schools, hospitals, and prisons, provides free USCF scholastic memberships for needy kids, supports selected national chess championships, and provides financial support for players who represent the United States in international competition. Donations to the U.S. Chess Trust are tax deductible. If you are a federal employee who donates to the Combined Federal Campaign, please select the U.S. Chess Trust as your chosen charity.

Q **How can I support U.S. chess?**

You can support chess in your community by donating your time to a local chess club. You can also support U.S. chess by making a tax-deductible donation to the U.S. Chess Trust. Donations are available at different levels. You can provide a chess set and board for a school, hospital, or prison; provide a USCF membership for one year for one child; or support the prize fund of the U.S. Blind Chess Championship; support one U.S. representative's participation in the World Youth Chess Championship. For details, please visit *www.uschess.org*.

Index

THE EVERYTHING SERIES!

BUSINESS & PERSONAL FINANCE

Everything® Accounting Book
Everything® Budgeting Book
Everything® Business Planning Book
Everything® Coaching and Mentoring Book
Everything® Fundraising Book
Everything® Get Out of Debt Book
Everything® Grant Writing Book
Everything® Guide to Personal Finance for Single Mothers
Everything® Home-Based Business Book, 2nd Ed.
Everything® Homebuying Book, 2nd Ed.
Everything® Homeselling Book, 2nd Ed.
Everything® Improve Your Credit Book
Everything® Investing Book, 2nd Ed.
Everything® Landlording Book
Everything® Leadership Book
Everything® Managing People Book, 2nd Ed.
Everything® Negotiating Book
Everything® Online Auctions Book
Everything® Online Business Book
Everything® Personal Finance Book
Everything® Personal Finance in Your 20s and 30s Book
Everything® Project Management Book
Everything® Real Estate Investing Book
Everything® Retirement Planning Book
Everything® Robert's Rules Book, $7.95
Everything® Selling Book
Everything® Start Your Own Business Book, 2nd Ed.
Everything® Wills & Estate Planning Book

COOKING

Everything® Barbecue Cookbook
Everything® Bartender's Book, $9.95
Everything® Cheese Book
Everything® Chinese Cookbook
Everything® Classic Recipes Book
Everything® Cocktail Parties and Drinks Book
Everything® College Cookbook
Everything® Cooking for Baby and Toddler Book
Everything® Cooking for Two Cookbook
Everything® Diabetes Cookbook
Everything® Easy Gourmet Cookbook
Everything® Fondue Cookbook
Everything® Fondue Party Book
Everything® Gluten-Free Cookbook
Everything® Glycemic Index Cookbook
Everything® Grilling Cookbook

Everything® Healthy Meals in Minutes Cookbook
Everything® Holiday Cookbook
Everything® Indian Cookbook
Everything® Italian Cookbook
Everything® Low-Carb Cookbook
Everything® Low-Fat High-Flavor Cookbook
Everything® Low-Salt Cookbook
Everything® Meals for a Month Cookbook
Everything® Mediterranean Cookbook
Everything® Mexican Cookbook
Everything® No Trans Fat Cookbook
Everything® One-Pot Cookbook
Everything® Pizza Cookbook
Everything® Quick and Easy 30-Minute, 5-Ingredient Cookbook
Everything® Quick Meals Cookbook
Everything® Slow Cooker Cookbook
Everything® Slow Cooking for a Crowd Cookbook
Everything® Soup Cookbook
Everything® Stir-Fry Cookbook
Everything® Tex-Mex Cookbook
Everything® Thai Cookbook
Everything® Vegetarian Cookbook
Everything® Wild Game Cookbook
Everything® Wine Book, 2nd Ed.

GAMES

Everything® 15-Minute Sudoku Book, $9.95
Everything® 30-Minute Sudoku Book, $9.95
Everything® Blackjack Strategy Book
Everything® Brain Strain Book, $9.95
Everything® Bridge Book
Everything® Card Games Book
Everything® Card Tricks Book, $9.95
Everything® Casino Gambling Book, 2nd Ed.
Everything® Chess Basics Book
Everything® Craps Strategy Book
Everything® Crossword and Puzzle Book
Everything® Crossword Challenge Book
Everything® Crosswords for the Beach Book, $9.95
Everything® Cryptograms Book, $9.95
Everything® Easy Crosswords Book
Everything® Easy Kakuro Book, $9.95
Everything® Easy Large Print Crosswords Book
Everything® Games Book, 2nd Ed.
Everything® Giant Sudoku Book, $9.95
Everything® Kakuro Challenge Book, $9.95
Everything® Large-Print Crossword Challenge Book

Everything® Large-Print Crosswords Book
Everything® Lateral Thinking Puzzles Book, $9.95
Everything® Mazes Book
Everything® Movie Crosswords Book, $9.95
Everything® Online Poker Book, $12.95
Everything® Pencil Puzzles Book, $9.95
Everything® Poker Strategy Book
Everything® Pool & Billiards Book
Everything® Sports Crosswords Book, $9.95
Everything® Test Your IQ Book, $9.95
Everything® Texas Hold 'Em Book, $9.95
Everything® Travel Crosswords Book, $9.95
Everything® Word Games Challenge Book
Everything® Word Scramble Book
Everything® Word Search Book

HEALTH

Everything® Alzheimer's Book
Everything® Diabetes Book
Everything® Health Guide to Adult Bipolar Disorder
Everything® Health Guide to Controlling Anxiety
Everything® Health Guide to Fibromyalgia
Everything® Health Guide to Postpartum Care
Everything® Health Guide to Thyroid Disease
Everything® Hypnosis Book
Everything® Low Cholesterol Book
Everything® Massage Book
Everything® Menopause Book
Everything® Nutrition Book
Everything® Reflexology Book
Everything® Stress Management Book

HISTORY

Everything® American Government Book
Everything® American History Book, 2nd Ed.
Everything® Civil War Book
Everything® Freemasons Book
Everything® Irish History & Heritage Book
Everything® Middle East Book

HOBBIES

Everything® Candlemaking Book
Everything® Cartooning Book
Everything® Coin Collecting Book
Everything® Drawing Book
Everything® Family Tree Book, 2nd Ed.
Everything® Knitting Book
Everything® Knots Book
Everything® Photography Book

Everything® Quilting Book
Everything® Scrapbooking Book
Everything® Sewing Book
Everything® Soapmaking Book, 2nd Ed.
Everything® Woodworking Book

HOME IMPROVEMENT

Everything® Feng Shui Book
Everything® Feng Shui Decluttering Book, $9.95
Everything® Fix-It Book
Everything® Home Decorating Book
Everything® Home Storage Solutions Book
Everything® Homebuilding Book
Everything® Organize Your Home Book

KIDS' BOOKS

All titles are $7.95
Everything® Kids' Animal Puzzle & Activity Book
Everything® Kids' Baseball Book, 4th Ed.
Everything® Kids' Bible Trivia Book
Everything® Kids' Bugs Book
Everything® Kids' Cars and Trucks Puzzle & Activity Book
Everything® Kids' Christmas Puzzle & Activity Book
Everything® Kids' Cookbook
Everything® Kids' Crazy Puzzles Book
Everything® Kids' Dinosaurs Book
Everything® Kids' First Spanish Puzzle and Activity Book
Everything® Kids' Gross Cookbook
Everything® Kids' Gross Hidden Pictures Book
Everything® Kids' Gross Jokes Book
Everything® Kids' Gross Mazes Book
Everything® Kids' Gross Puzzle and Activity Book
Everything® Kids' Halloween Puzzle & Activity Book
Everything® Kids' Hidden Pictures Book
Everything® Kids' Horses Book
Everything® Kids' Joke Book
Everything® Kids' Knock Knock Book
Everything® Kids' Learning Spanish Book
Everything® Kids' Math Puzzles Book
Everything® Kids' Mazes Book
Everything® Kids' Money Book
Everything® Kids' Nature Book
Everything® Kids' Pirates Puzzle and Activity Book
Everything® Kids' Presidents Book
Everything® Kids' Princess Puzzle and Activity Book
Everything® Kids' Puzzle Book
Everything® Kids' Riddles & Brain Teasers Book
Everything® Kids' Science Experiments Book
Everything® Kids' Sharks Book
Everything® Kids' Soccer Book
Everything® Kids' States Book
Everything® Kids' Travel Activity Book

KIDS' STORY BOOKS

Everything® Fairy Tales Book

LANGUAGE

Everything® Conversational Japanese Book with CD, $19.95
Everything® French Grammar Book
Everything® French Phrase Book, $9.95
Everything® French Verb Book, $9.95
Everything® German Practice Book with CD, $19.95
Everything® Inglés Book
Everything® Intermediate Spanish Book with CD, $19.95
Everything® Learning Brazilian Portuguese Book with CD, $19.95
Everything® Learning French Book
Everything® Learning German Book
Everything® Learning Italian Book
Everything® Learning Latin Book
Everything® Learning Spanish Book with CD, 2nd Edition, $19.95
Everything® Russian Practice Book with CD, $19.95
Everything® Sign Language Book
Everything® Spanish Grammar Book
Everything® Spanish Phrase Book, $9.95
Everything® Spanish Practice Book with CD, $19.95
Everything® Spanish Verb Book, $9.95
Everything® Speaking Mandarin Chinese Book with CD, $19.95

MUSIC

Everything® Drums Book with CD, $19.95
Everything® Guitar Book with CD, 2nd Edition, $19.95
Everything® Guitar Chords Book with CD, $19.95
Everything® Home Recording Book
Everything® Music Theory Book with CD, $19.95
Everything® Reading Music Book with CD, $19.95
Everything® Rock & Blues Guitar Book with CD, $19.95
Everything® Rock and Blues Piano Book with CD, $19.95
Everything® Songwriting Book

NEW AGE

Everything® Astrology Book, 2nd Ed.
Everything® Birthday Personology Book
Everything® Dreams Book, 2nd Ed.
Everything® Love Signs Book, $9.95
Everything® Numerology Book
Everything® Paganism Book
Everything® Palmistry Book
Everything® Psychic Book
Everything® Reiki Book

Everything® Sex Signs Book, $9.95
Everything® Tarot Book, 2nd Ed.
Everything® Toltec Wisdom Book
Everything® Wicca and Witchcraft Book

PARENTING

Everything® Baby Names Book, 2nd Ed.
Everything® Baby Shower Book
Everything® Baby's First Year Book
Everything® Birthing Book
Everything® Breastfeeding Book
Everything® Father-to-Be Book
Everything® Father's First Year Book
Everything® Get Ready for Baby Book
Everything® Get Your Baby to Sleep Book, $9.95
Everything® Getting Pregnant Book
Everything® Guide to Raising a One-Year-Old
Everything® Guide to Raising a Two-Year-Old
Everything® Homeschooling Book
Everything® Mother's First Year Book
Everything® Parent's Guide to Childhood Illnesses
Everything® Parent's Guide to Children and Divorce
Everything® Parent's Guide to Children with ADD/ADHD
Everything® Parent's Guide to Children with Asperger's Syndrome
Everything® Parent's Guide to Children with Autism
Everything® Parent's Guide to Children with Bipolar Disorder
Everything® Parent's Guide to Children with Depression
Everything® Parent's Guide to Children with Dyslexia
Everything® Parent's Guide to Children with Juvenile Diabetes
Everything® Parent's Guide to Positive Discipline
Everything® Parent's Guide to Raising a Successful Child
Everything® Parent's Guide to Raising Boys
Everything® Parent's Guide to Raising Girls
Everything® Parent's Guide to Raising Siblings
Everything® Parent's Guide to Sensory Integration Disorder
Everything® Parent's Guide to Tantrums
Everything® Parent's Guide to the Strong-Willed Child
Everything® Parenting a Teenager Book
Everything® Potty Training Book, $9.95
Everything® Pregnancy Book, 3rd Ed.
Everything® Pregnancy Fitness Book
Everything® Pregnancy Nutrition Book
Everything® Pregnancy Organizer, 2nd Ed., $16.95
Everything® Toddler Activities Book
Everything® Toddler Book

Everything® Tween Book
Everything® Twins, Triplets, and More Book

PETS

Everything® Aquarium Book
Everything® Boxer Book
Everything® Cat Book, 2nd Ed.
Everything® Chihuahua Book
Everything® Dachshund Book
Everything® Dog Book
Everything® Dog Health Book
Everything® Dog Obedience Book
Everything® Dog Owner's Organizer, $16.95
Everything® Dog Training and Tricks Book
Everything® German Shepherd Book
Everything® Golden Retriever Book
Everything® Horse Book
Everything® Horse Care Book
Everything® Horseback Riding Book
Everything® Labrador Retriever Book
Everything® Poodle Book
Everything® Pug Book
Everything® Puppy Book
Everything® Rottweiler Book
Everything® Small Dogs Book
Everything® Tropical Fish Book
Everything® Yorkshire Terrier Book

REFERENCE

Everything® American Presidents Book
Everything® Blogging Book
Everything® Build Your Vocabulary Book
Everything® Car Care Book
Everything® Classical Mythology Book
Everything® Da Vinci Book
Everything® Divorce Book
Everything® Einstein Book
Everything® Enneagram Book
Everything® Etiquette Book, 2nd Ed.
Everything® Inventions and Patents Book
Everything® Mafia Book
Everything® Philosophy Book
Everything® Pirates Book
Everything® Psychology Book

RELIGION

Everything® Angels Book
Everything® Bible Book
Everything® Buddhism Book
Everything® Catholicism Book
Everything® Christianity Book
Everything® Gnostic Gospels Book
Everything® History of the Bible Book
Everything® Jesus Book

Everything® Jewish History & Heritage Book
Everything® Judaism Book
Everything® Kabbalah Book
Everything® Koran Book
Everything® Mary Book
Everything® Mary Magdalene Book
Everything® Prayer Book
Everything® Saints Book, 2nd Ed.
Everything® Torah Book
Everything® Understanding Islam Book
Everything® World's Religions Book
Everything® Zen Book

SCHOOL & CAREERS

Everything® Alternative Careers Book
Everything® Career Tests Book
Everything® College Major Test Book
Everything® College Survival Book, 2nd Ed.
Everything® Cover Letter Book, 2nd Ed.
Everything® Filmmaking Book
Everything® Get-a-Job Book, 2nd Ed.
Everything® Guide to Being a Paralegal
Everything® Guide to Being a Personal Trainer
Everything® Guide to Being a Real Estate Agent
Everything® Guide to Being a Sales Rep
Everything® Guide to Careers in Health Care
Everything® Guide to Careers in Law Enforcement
Everything® Guide to Government Jobs
Everything® Guide to Starting and Running a Restaurant
Everything® Job Interview Book
Everything® New Nurse Book
Everything® New Teacher Book
Everything® Paying for College Book
Everything® Practice Interview Book
Everything® Resume Book, 2nd Ed.
Everything® Study Book

SELF-HELP

Everything® Dating Book, 2nd Ed.
Everything® Great Sex Book
Everything® Self-Esteem Book
Everything® Tantric Sex Book

SPORTS & FITNESS

Everything® Easy Fitness Book
Everything® Running Book
Everything® Weight Training Book

TRAVEL

Everything® Family Guide to Cruise Vacations
Everything® Family Guide to Hawaii
Everything® Family Guide to Las Vegas, 2nd Ed.
Everything® Family Guide to Mexico
Everything® Family Guide to New York City, 2nd Ed.
Everything® Family Guide to RV Travel & Campgrounds
Everything® Family Guide to the Caribbean
Everything® Family Guide to the Walt Disney World Resort®, Universal Studios®, and Greater Orlando, 4th Ed.
Everything® Family Guide to Timeshares
Everything® Family Guide to Washington D.C., 2nd Ed.

WEDDINGS

Everything® Bachelorette Party Book, $9.95
Everything® Bridesmaid Book, $9.95
Everything® Destination Wedding Book
Everything® Elopement Book, $9.95
Everything® Father of the Bride Book, $9.95
Everything® Groom Book, $9.95
Everything® Mother of the Bride Book, $9.95
Everything® Outdoor Wedding Book
Everything® Wedding Book, 3rd Ed.
Everything® Wedding Checklist, $9.95
Everything® Wedding Etiquette Book, $9.95
Everything® Wedding Organizer, 2nd Ed., $16.95
Everything® Wedding Shower Book, $9.95
Everything® Wedding Vows Book, $9.95
Everything® Wedding Workout Book
Everything® Weddings on a Budget Book, $9.95

WRITING

Everything® Creative Writing Book
Everything® Get Published Book, 2nd Ed.
Everything® Grammar and Style Book
Everything® Guide to Magazine Writing
Everything® Guide to Writing a Book Proposal
Everything® Guide to Writing a Novel
Everything® Guide to Writing Children's Books
Everything® Guide to Writing Copy
Everything® Guide to Writing Research Papers
Everything® Screenwriting Book
Everything® Writing Poetry Book
Everything® Writing Well Book